SOURDOUGH MADE PERFECT

1000 Days to Unlock the Secrets of Baking Incredible Bread and Discover a World of Culinary Possibilities

PATRICIA C. MEADORS

EDITOR: LYN
INTERIOR DESIGN: FAIZAN
COVER ART: ABR
FOOD STYLIST: JO

Table of Contents

Introduction

Today, I want to introduce you to a world of culinary enchantment that goes beyond words—an adventure in sourdough bread-making.

Sourdough is a type of bread made through the fermentation of dough using naturally occurring yeast and bacteria. It has a distinct tangy flavor and a chewy texture. Sourdough bread is often prized for its depth of flavor and the complexity it adds to various recipes.

Sourdough bread has been around for thousands of years and is believed to be one of the oldest forms of leavened bread. The process begins by combining flour and water to create a starter. This mixture is then left to ferment at room temperature, allowing wild yeast and lactobacilli bacteria present in the environment to colonize the starter. Over time, the starter develops a complex ecosystem of microorganisms, which give the bread its unique flavor and texture.

The process of making sourdough involves creating a starter, which is a mixture of flour and water that captures wild yeast and bacteria from the environment. This starter is then used to leaven the bread dough. Sourdough fermentation can take longer than traditional bread-making methods because it relies on the natural fermentation process.

Sourdough bread is known for its health benefits as well. The fermentation process breaks down some of the gluten in the bread, making it easier to digest for some individuals. Additionally, sourdough bread has a lower glycemic index compared to regular bread, which means it doesn't cause a rapid spike in blood sugar levels.

Imagine a process that combines science, artistry, and tradition to create loaves that are not just bread, but edible masterpieces. Sourdough bread is crafted through the alchemy of wild yeast and bacteria, transforming simple ingredients into a symphony of flavors. The result is a bread with a tangy depth, a chewy texture, and a crust that sings when you bite into it.

But sourdough is not just about the end product—it is about the journey itself. It is a chance to delve into the realm of fermentation, to witness the magic of a living starter transforming flour and water into a thriving ecosystem. It is an opportunity to nurture, experiment, and unleash your creativity through kneading, shaping, and scoring.

Beyond its sheer delight for the senses, sourdough bread holds health benefits that are both intriguing and remarkable. The fermentation process breaks down complex carbohydrates and gluten, making it potentially more digestible and gentle on the stomach. Moreover, the nutrients within the bread become more bioavailable, nourishing both body and soul.

Chapter 1
The Science and Superiority of Sourdough

What Is Sourdough Starter?

A sourdough starter, also known as a sourdough culture or levain, is a mixture of flour and water that captures wild yeast and bacteria from the environment. It serves as the leavening agent in sourdough bread-making. A sourdough starter is essentially a living ecosystem of microorganisms that ferment the dough, giving it the distinct flavor, texture, and rise characteristic of sourdough bread.

Here are the details of what a sourdough starter entails:

INGREDIENTS

A basic sourdough starter requires two primary ingredients: flour and water. Typically, equal parts of flour (such as wheat, rye, or a combination) and water are used to create the initial mixture. The flour provides nutrients for the microorganisms, while the water hydrates the mixture and creates an environment for fermentation to occur.

WILD YEAST AND BACTERIA

The key component of a sourdough starter is the wild yeast and lactic acid bacteria present in the environment. These microorganisms are naturally occurring and can be found on the surface of grains, fruits, and in the air. When mixed with flour and water, the microorganisms begin to colonize and thrive within the mixture, initiating the fermentation process.

FERMENTATION

Over time, the wild yeast and bacteria in the starter consume the carbohydrates in the flour, producing carbon dioxide gas and organic acids. This process of fermentation causes the dough to rise and develop the characteristic tangy flavor of sourdough bread. The fermentation also helps break down complex carbohydrates and gluten in the dough, making it more digestible.

FEEDING AND MAINTENANCE

To keep the sourdough starter active and healthy, it requires regular feeding. Feeding involves discarding a portion of the starter and replenishing it with fresh flour and water. This process helps maintain the balance of microorganisms, prevents the starter from becoming too acidic, and provides fresh nutrients for the microorganisms to thrive.

DEVELOPMENT AND MATURATION

A new sourdough starter requires time to develop and mature. Initially, it may take several days of regular feedings and care to establish a strong and active culture. As the starter matures, the flavors and fermentation activity intensify, resulting in more complex and flavorful bread.

Each sourdough starter is unique, influenced by the specific environment, flour types, and feeding routine. Some bakers have cherished starters that have been passed down through generations, each carrying a distinct lineage and flavor profile.

Creating and maintaining a sourdough starter is a rewarding process that requires attention, patience, and experimentation. Once established, a well-maintained starter can be used indefinitely, providing a reliable source of leavening for sourdough bread and other fermented baked goods.

How Sourdough Works

Sourdough works through a process called fermentation, which involves the interaction between wild yeast, bacteria, flour, and water. Here's a step-by-step explanation of how sourdough works:

CAPTURE WILD YEAST AND BACTERIA

To create a sourdough starter, you mix flour and water together and let it sit in a warm environment. The mixture attracts wild yeast and bacteria naturally present in the environment. These microorganisms begin to colonize and feed on the carbohydrates present in the flour.

FERMENTATION

As the wild yeast and bacteria consume the carbohydrates in the flour, they produce two key byproducts: carbon dioxide and organic acids. The carbon dioxide gas gets trapped in the dough, causing it to rise and giving the bread its airy texture. The organic acids, particularly lactic and acetic acids, contribute to the distinctive tangy flavor of sourdough bread.

GLUTEN DEVELOPMENT

Sourdough fermentation also affects gluten, a protein found in wheat and other grains. The organic acids produced during fermentation help break down gluten strands, making them more easily digestible for some individuals. This process contributes to the chewy texture of sourdough bread.

FLAVOR AND AROMA DEVELOPMENT

The longer the fermentation process, the more pronounced the flavor and aroma of the sourdough bread. The organic acids and other compounds produced during fermentation add complexity and depth to the taste profile, creating the characteristic tanginess and rich flavors associated with sourdough.

NUTRIENT TRANSFORMATION

Fermentation in sourdough also leads to the breakdown of phytic acid, an antinutrient found in grains. Phytic acid can inhibit the absorption of certain minerals. However, the fermentation process helps reduce phytic acid levels, making the minerals in the bread more bioavailable and easier for our bodies to absorb.

LEAVENING AGENT

In traditional bread-making, commercial yeast is used as a leavening agent to make the dough rise. In sourdough, the wild yeast in the starter serves as the natural leavening agent. The wild yeast feeds on the carbohydrates in the dough, releasing carbon dioxide gas, which creates bubbles and causes the dough to rise.

Benefits of Sourdough fermentation

Sourdough fermentation has several benefits that make it a popular choice for bread-making and contribute to its reputation for being more digestible and nutritious compared to bread made with commercial yeast. Here are some key points to expand on:

IMPROVED DIGESTIBILITY

The fermentation process of sourdough helps to break down complex carbohydrates and proteins in the bread. This process pre-digests the starches and gluten, making them easier for our bodies to digest. The bacteria and yeast in the sourdough starter produce enzymes that break down these components, resulting in a bread that may be better tolerated by individuals with gluten sensitivities or digestive issues.

ENHANCED NUTRIENT AVAILABILITY

Sourdough fermentation can increase the availability and absorption of certain nutrients present in the bread. The beneficial bacteria in the starter culture produce enzymes that break down phytic acid, a natural compound found in grains. Phytic acid can inhibit the absorption of minerals like iron, zinc, and calcium. By reducing phytic acid levels, sourdough fermentation makes these minerals more bioavailable and easier for our bodies to absorb.

LOWER GLYCEMIC INDEX

Sourdough bread generally has a lower glycemic index (GI) compared to bread made with commercial yeast. The GI is a measure of how quickly a carbohydrate-containing food raises blood sugar levels. Sourdough fermentation slows down the digestion and absorption of carbohydrates, resulting in a slower release of glucose into the bloodstream. This can help regulate blood sugar levels, making sourdough bread a favorable option for people concerned about their blood sugar control.

NATURAL PRESERVATIVE PROPERTIES

Sourdough bread tends to have a longer shelf life compared to bread made with commercial yeast. The acetic acid produced during fermentation acts as a natural preservative, inhibiting the growth of mold and prolonging the freshness of the bread without the need for artificial additives or preservatives.

Troubleshooting

SLUGGISH STARTER

If your starter is not showing much activity or taking a long time to rise, it may need more frequent feedings or a warmer environment. Try feeding your starter more often (every 8-12 hours) and placing it in a slightly warmer spot, such as near a warm oven or on top of a fridge.

NO RISE OR POOR OVEN SPRING

If your dough is not rising properly during fermentation or doesn't spring up in the oven, it may be due to weak or inactive yeast. Check the vitality of your starter by performing a float test: drop a small spoonful of starter into a glass of water; if it floats, it's active and ready to use. If it sinks, you may need to feed your starter more regularly or increase its hydration.

DENSE OR GUMMY CRUMB

If your sourdough bread has a dense or gummy crumb, it may be a sign of underproofing or overproofing. Underproofing occurs when the dough hasn't had enough time to fully rise before baking, while overproofing happens when the dough has fermented for too long. Pay attention to the dough's volume and structure during proofing, and adjust the fermentation time accordingly.

LACK OF OVEN SPRING

If your dough doesn't get that desired burst of rise in the oven, it could be due to insufficient gluten development or not enough steam during baking. Ensure that you adequately knead the dough to develop gluten, and consider using steam in the oven by placing a tray of hot water or using a spray bottle to create a moist environment.

EXCESSIVE SOURNESS

If your sourdough bread tastes overly sour, it may be a result of an extended fermentation period or a high proportion of whole grain flour. Shortening the fermentation time or reducing the amount of whole grain flour in your recipe can help balance the sourness.

SOURDOUGH BREAD COLLAPSING

If your bread rises well during fermentation but collapses or deflates during baking, it could be due to inadequate gluten development, weak structure, or excessive moisture in the dough. Ensure you have properly kneaded the dough and that it has sufficient strength before shaping. Adjust the hydration level of the dough if necessary.

Chapter 2
Start With Your Starter

Starter Step by Step

DAY 1:

In a clean container, combine 50 grams of whole wheat flour and 50 grams of water. Using whole wheat flour at the beginning provides more nutrients for the yeast and bacteria.

Stir well to create a thick batter, making sure there are no dry clumps of flour.

Cover the container loosely with a clean kitchen towel or plastic wrap. This allows airflow while preventing any contaminants from entering.

Let the starter sit at room temperature (around 70-75°F or 21-24°C) for 24 hours. This gives time for the natural yeast and bacteria present in the flour and the environment to begin colonizing the mixture.

DAY 2:

Observe the starter for any signs of activity. Look for small bubbles on the surface or an increase in volume. If there are no visible signs of activity yet, don't worry, as it can take a few days for the fermentation process to kick in.

Discard and remove about half of the starter (approximately 50 grams) from the container. This helps control the volume and maintain a manageable size for future feedings.

Add 50 grams of whole wheat flour and 50 grams of water to the remaining starter. This feeding provides fresh food for the microorganisms to consume and thrive.

Stir well to incorporate the fresh flour and water into the starter, ensuring a consistent texture.

Cover the container and let it sit at room temperature for another 24 hours. This allows the newly added food to be consumed and further fermentation to occur.

DAY 3:

Repeat the observation process, looking for signs of activity. You may start noticing small bubbles forming and a slightly sour aroma developing.

Discard and remove about half of the starter (approximately 50 grams) as before.

Add 50 grams of all-purpose flour and 50 grams of water to the remaining starter. Transitioning to all-purpose flour makes it easier for the starter to become more active and accessible to a wider range of recipes.

Stir well to incorporate the fresh flour and water into the starter.

Cover and let it sit at room temperature for 24 hours to continue the fermentation process.

DAY 4:

Continue observing for signs of activity, such as increased bubbling and a pleasant sour aroma. The starter should start showing more significant signs of fermentation.

Discard and remove about half of the starter (approximately 50 grams).

Add 50 grams of all-purpose flour and 50 grams of water to the remaining starter.

Stir well to incorporate the fresh flour and water into the starter.

Cover and let it sit at room temperature for 24 hours, allowing the fermentation to progress further.

DAY 5:

Repeat the observation process, looking for increased signs of fermentation. The starter should exhibit more bubbles and may rise and fall noticeably.
Discard and remove about half of the starter (approximately 50 grams).

Add 50 grams of all-purpose flour and 50 grams of water to the remaining starter.

Stir well to incorporate the fresh flour and water into the starter.

Cover and let it sit at room temperature for 24 hours, continuing to develop the sourdough culture.

DAY 6:

Continue observing the starter for further signs of activity, such as vigorous bubbling and a pleasant sour aroma. The starter should start to become more active and show more consistent signs of fermentation.

Discard and remove about half of the starter (approximately 50 grams).

Add 50 grams of all-purpose flour and 50 grams of water to the remaining starter.

Stir well to incorporate the fresh flour and water into the starter.

Cover and let it sit at room temperature for 24 hours, allowing the fermentation process to mature.

DAY 7:

Observe the starter's activity, noting if it consistently doubles in volume within 6-8 hours of feeding. This indicates that the starter is now active and capable of leavening bread.

If the starter is consistently active and showing signs of fermentation, it is ready to use in your sourdough bread recipes.

Remember to continue regular feedings and maintenance to keep the starter healthy and active.

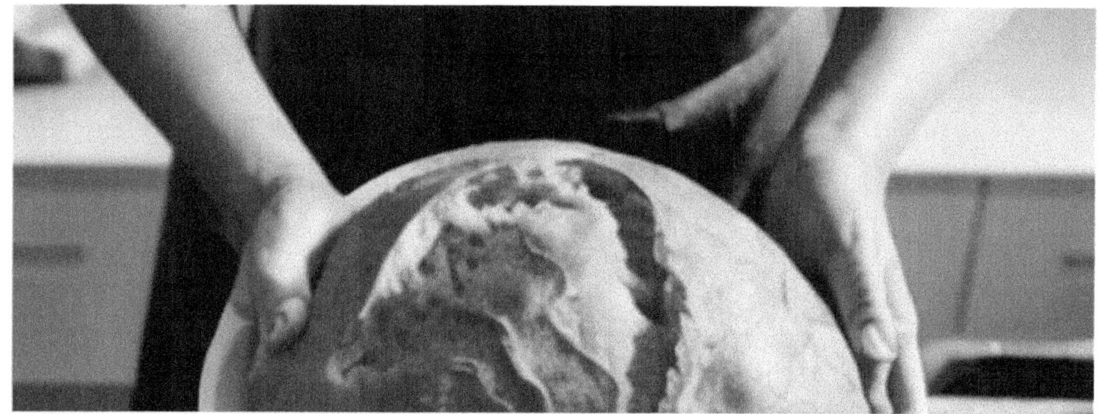

By following this detailed day-by-day process, you can establish a strong and active sourdough starter ready for baking delicious bread. Remember, the fermentation process can be influenced by various factors, so don't worry if your starter takes a bit longer to develop. Patience and careful observation will lead to a successful sourdough starter.

Drying and Reactivating the Sourdough Starter

DRYING THE STARTER

To dry your sourdough starter, begin by spreading a thin layer of active starter on a piece of parchment paper or a silicone baking mat. Allow it to dry completely at room temperature. This process can take several days, so make sure it is fully dried before moving on to the next step.

STORING THE DRIED STARTER

Once the starter is completely dry, you can store it in an airtight container or a resealable bag. Keep it in a cool, dry place until you are ready to reactivate it.

Reactivating the Dry Sourdough Starter

REHYDRATING THE STARTER

Take a small portion of the dried starter and mix it with an equal amount of flour and water. For example, if you have 10 grams of dried starter, add 10 grams of flour and 10 grams of water. Stir well to combine and let it sit at room temperature for a few hours.

FEEDING THE STARTER

After the initial rehydration, discard a portion of the starter (to keep the volume manageable) and add fresh flour and water in a 1:1:1 ratio. For example, if you have 20 grams of rehydrated starter, discard 10 grams and add 10 grams each of flour and water. Mix well and let it sit at room temperature.

DAILY FEEDINGS

Repeat the process of discarding a portion of the starter and feeding it with fresh flour and water in a 1:1:1 ratio once or twice a day. This helps establish a healthy population of yeast and bacteria in the starter, allowing it to become active and vigorous again.

Long-Term Storage

STORING THE STARTER IN THE REFRIGERATOR

Once your sourdough starter is active and well-established, you can store it in the refrigerator for long-term storage. Before refrigerating, feed the starter with fresh flour and water to ensure it has enough food to sustain it during the dormant period.

FEEDING THE REFRIGERATED STARTER

While in the refrigerator, the sourdough starter can be fed once a week to keep it healthy and active. Discard a portion of the starter and add fresh flour and water in a 1:1:1 ratio, mixing well. Return the container to the refrigerator until the next feeding.

Bringing the Starter out of Refrigeration: When you want to use the starter, take it out of the refrigerator and let it come to room temperature. Feed it with fresh flour and water, discarding a portion as necessary to maintain the desired volume. Allow the starter to become active and bubbly before using it in your sourdough bread recipe.

Chapter 3
Prepare Your Kitchen for Your First Bake

A Starter Kitchen

INGREDIENTS:

- Flour: Choose high-quality flours, such as all-purpose flour, whole wheat flour, or bread flour. These flours provide the nutrients necessary for a healthy starter.
- Water: Use filtered or bottled water, free from chlorine or other chemicals that might inhibit fermentation.
- Salt: Good quality sea salt or kosher salt for bread recipes.

EQUIPMENT:

- Mixing bowls: Have a set of mixing bowls in different sizes to accommodate various steps of the baking process.
- Measuring tools: Use a digital kitchen scale for precise measurements by weight, as it is more accurate than measuring by volume.
- Utensils: Gather a dough scraper, a whisk or spoon for mixing, and a spatula for folding and shaping dough.
- Baking vessels: Depending on the type of bread you plan to bake, consider having a Dutch oven, baking stone, or bread loaf pans.
- Oven thermometer: Ensure your oven temperature is accurate for consistent baking results.
- Cooling rack: Allow your bread to cool evenly by placing it on a cooling rack after baking.

STORAGE AND FERMENTATION:

- Glass jars or containers: Use glass jars or food-safe containers to store your sourdough starter and for bulk fermentation.
- Kitchen towels and plastic wrap: Cover your dough during fermentation to prevent it from drying out.
- Proofing baskets: These baskets, also known as bannetons, help shape the dough and provide structure during the final rise.

MAINTENANCE AND CARE:

- Feeding schedule: Establish a regular feeding schedule for your sourdough starter, typically once or twice a day depending on your baking frequency.
- Discard container: Keep a container specifically for discarding excess starter during feedings.
- Refrigerator space: Reserve space in your refrigerator to store the sourdough starter if you plan to keep it dormant between baking sessions.

LEARNING RESOURCES:

- Books and recipes: Collect reputable sourdough baking books and recipes to learn various techniques and expand your knowledge.
- Online communities: Join online forums or social media groups dedicated to sourdough baking, where you can share experiences, ask questions, and gain valuable insights.

Remember, building a starter kitchen is a gradual process. Start with the essentials and gradually add tools and ingredients based on your baking preferences and needs. As you gain more experience, you can explore additional equipment and experiment with different flours and recipes.

Getting Ready for Your First Bake

ENSURE YOUR SOURDOUGH STARTER IS HEALTHY AND ACTIVE

It's essential to ensure that your sourdough starter is active and vibrant before using it in your bake.

Feed your starter at its peak activity, when it has doubled in size and is showing consistent signs of fermentation.

This usually occurs 4-6 hours after a feeding.

Using a well-fed starter with active yeast and bacteria will help your dough rise properly and develop desirable flavors.

Embrace Precision: Measure Ingredients by Weight
Measuring ingredients by weight rather than volume is crucial for consistent and accurate results.

Different flours have varying densities, so measuring by weight ensures you're using the correct ratios.

Use a digital kitchen scale to weigh your ingredients, including flour, water, and salt. This precision helps maintain the right hydration level and dough consistency.

HARNESS THE POWER OF WATER TEMPERATURE

Water temperature affects the fermentation process, as it activates the yeast and bacteria in the starter.

Ideally, the water temperature should be between 75°F to 85°F (24°C to 29°C) for most sourdough recipes.

Warmer water speeds up fermentation, while cooler water slows it down. Adjust the water temperature based on the desired fermentation timeline and ambient conditions.

Create the Ideal Environment: Understanding the Importance of Air Temperature

The ambient temperature of your kitchen plays a crucial role in the fermentation process and flavor development.

Different temperatures can impact the activity of the yeast and bacteria in your dough.

If your kitchen is cooler, fermentation may take longer. Consider creating a warmer environment by using your oven with the light turned on or placing the dough in a slightly warmed room.

Time: The Secret Ingredient in Sourdough Baking

Time is a vital ingredient in sourdough baking, affecting flavor development, dough structure, and texture.

Follow the recipe's suggested timeframes as a starting point, but also use your judgment and observation.

Pay attention to the appearance and behavior of your dough throughout the fermentation and proofing stages. Adjust the timeframes based on your dough's readiness and desired flavors.

Step by Step Bread Baking

AUTOLYSE:

Autolyse is a technique that involves mixing flour and water and allowing them to rest for a period of time, typically 30 minutes to an hour. During this time, the flour hydrates and begins to absorb the water, which kickstarts enzyme activity. This enzymatic activity helps break down complex carbohydrates, improving the dough's extensibility and promoting better gluten development. Autolysing the dough can lead to a more open crumb structure, improved flavor, and easier handling during the later stages of bread making. To autolyse, simply combine the flour and water in a bowl until no dry spots remain, cover it, and let it rest.

Tip: Use a large mixing bowl to give your dough enough space to expand during fermentation.

MIXING:

Mixing is the process of incorporating the sourdough starter and salt into the autolysed dough. Use a dough scraper or your hands to bring all the ingredients together. Mixing thoroughly ensures even distribution of the starter and salt throughout the dough, allowing for consistent fermentation and flavor development. Avoid excessive kneading at this stage, as it can lead to excessive gluten development and a denser texture in the final loaf. Mix until all the ingredients are well incorporated and no dry spots or lumps of flour remain.

Tip: Use a dough scraper or your hands to incorporate the sourdough starter and salt into the autolysed dough.

GLUTEN DEVELOPMENT:

Gluten development is a critical step in bread baking, as it gives the dough structure and elasticity. There are different methods to develop gluten, such as kneading or folding. For novice bakers, the folding method is recommended. After mixing, let the dough rest for a few minutes, then perform a series of gentle stretch and folds. This involves grabbing one side of the dough, stretching it, and folding it over the center. Repeat this process several times, rotating the dough as you go. The folding action helps align the gluten strands, creating a strong and elastic dough. Repeat the folding process at regular intervals during the bulk fermentation stage to further strengthen the gluten network.

Tip: For novice bakers, it's recommended to start with the folding method, which involves gently stretching and folding the dough.

BULK FERMENTATION OR FIRST RISE:

Bulk fermentation is the stage where the dough undergoes its primary fermentation. During this time, the yeast and bacteria present in the sourdough starter metabolize the sugars in the dough, producing carbon dioxide gas, which causes the dough to rise. This fermentation stage is essential for flavor development. To achieve optimal fermentation, place the dough in a large bowl, cover it with a damp cloth or plastic wrap, and let it rest at room temperature. The duration of the bulk fermentation can vary depending on factors such as temperature, starter activity, and recipe. It typically lasts around 3 to 4 hours but can be extended up to 6 hours or longer in some cases. Monitor the dough's progress by observing its rise and checking for air bubbles.

Tip: Find a warm spot in your kitchen for the dough to ferment. You can place it near a window or use the oven with the light turned on (but not the heat).

PRESHAPING:

Preshaping is a crucial step that helps prepare the dough for its final shaping. It involves gently shaping the fermented dough into a round or rectangular shape, known as a boule or batard. Preshaping helps create tension on the dough's surface, which contributes to a better rise and shape during the final proof. To preshape, carefully transfer the dough to a lightly floured work surface. Use a bench scraper or your hands to gently fold the edges of the dough towards the center, creating tension on the surface. Rotate the dough as you go to ensure even shaping. Be gentle to preserve the gas bubbles formed during fermentation.

Tip: Lightly flour your work surface to prevent the dough from sticking while shaping.

BENCH REST:

After preshaping, the dough requires a short bench rest to relax before the final shaping. This rest period allows the gluten strands to relax, making the dough easier to work with during shaping. Simply cover the preshaped dough with a clean kitchen towel or plastic wrap and let it rest on the work surface for around 15 to 30 minutes. The bench rest also helps the dough retain its shape during the final shaping stage. While the dough is resting, use this time to prepare any shaping tools, such as a proofing basket or a baking sheet, and lightly dust them with flour to prevent sticking.

Tip: Cover the dough with a clean kitchen towel or plastic wrap during the bench rest to prevent it from drying out.

SHAPING

Shaping is the process of creating the final desired shape for the dough. There are various shaping techniques, and the choice depends on the type of loaf you want to achieve. For a boule (round loaf), gently cup your hands around the dough and use your thumbs to create tension on the surface while rotating the dough in a circular motion. For a batard (oval loaf), fold the dough in half lengthwise and seal the edges by pinching them together. Then, roll the dough gently while applying slight pressure to elongate it. As a novice baker, it's helpful to watch video tutorials or follow step-by-step instructions with visuals to master shaping techniques. Practice and patience are key to improving your shaping skills.

Tip: Watch video tutorials or seek visual references to learn different shaping techniques, such as shaping a boule or batard.

FINAL PROOF OR SECOND RISE

The final proof is the last fermentation stage before baking, where the shaped dough undergoes its second rise. This allows the yeast to continue producing carbon dioxide and for the dough to further develop its flavor and texture. Place the shaped dough in a proofing basket or on a baking sheet, seam side up, and cover it loosely with a kitchen towel or plastic wrap. The duration of the final proof depends on factors like temperature and the desired level of fermentation. It typically ranges from 1 to 2 hours, but it can be longer if the dough is cold or if a slower rise is desired. Monitor the dough's progress by observing its rise and checking for a slight jiggle when gently tapped.

Tip: Use a proofing basket or line a bowl with a well-floured kitchen towel to help the dough maintain its shape during the final rise.

BROWNING

Achieving a beautiful golden brown crust is a desirable characteristic of sourdough bread. Proper browning occurs due to Maillard reactions, which are enhanced by the presence of sugars and proteins on the surface of the dough. To promote browning, preheat your oven at the recommended temperature. You can also use techniques like the Dutch oven method or baking on a preheated baking stone to create a hot baking environment that encourages browning. Additionally, introducing steam into the oven during the initial stages of baking helps create a moist environment and enhances crust development. This can be done by placing a pan of hot water in the bottom of the oven or by spraying the oven walls with water.

Tip: Preheat your oven with a baking stone or a Dutch oven inside to create a hot baking environment for a well-browned crust.

SCORING

Scoring is the process of making shallow cuts on the surface of the dough just before baking. These cuts serve several purposes, including controlling the direction of the dough's expansion and allowing steam to escape during baking. Proper scoring helps create an even rise and a visually appealing pattern on the crust. To score, use a sharp blade or a bread lame and hold it at a shallow angle to the surface of the dough. Make swift, confident cuts, but avoid pressing too deeply to prevent deflating the dough. Experiment with different scoring patterns, such as straight lines, crosses, or decorative designs, to add a personal touch to your loaves.

Tip: Use a sharp blade or a bread lame to make quick, shallow cuts on the surface of the dough.

BAKING

Baking is the final step in the sourdough bread-making process. Preheat your oven to the recommended temperature, ensuring it reaches the desired heat before placing the dough inside. The baking time can vary depending on factors like oven temperature, loaf size, and recipe instructions. It usually ranges from 30 to 45 minutes. During the first half of baking, steam plays a crucial role in crust formation and oven spring (the rapid rise of the dough). You can create steam by placing a pan of hot water in the oven or by using a spray bottle to mist the oven walls. After the initial steam phase, remove the water source to allow the crust to dry and develop a crispy texture.

Tip: Follow the recommended baking temperature and time in your recipe, but adjust as needed based on your oven's behavior.

COOLING

Once the bread is baked, resist the temptation to cut into it immediately. Cooling is an important step for the bread's texture and flavor development. Transfer the baked loaf to a wire rack and let it cool completely. Cooling typically takes 2 to 3 hours, allowing the internal moisture to redistribute, the crumb to set, and the flavors to fully develop. Cutting into a hot loaf can result in a gummy texture, and the flavors may not be fully balanced. Patience is key to achieving the best results. Enjoy the delightful aroma filling your kitchen as the bread cools.

Tip: It's tempting to slice into freshly baked bread, but allowing it to cool completely ensures a better texture and flavor.

SERVING

Finally, it's time to enjoy your homemade sourdough bread. Once the loaf has cooled completely, slice it using a sharp bread knife. Sourdough bread is delicious on its own, but it also pairs well with a variety of spreads, such as butter, jam, cheese, or avocado. Get creative and explore different flavor combinations to enhance your sourdough experience.

Tip: Freshly baked sourdough is delicious on its own, but it also pairs well with spreads like butter, jam, or cheese.

STORAGE

To keep your bread fresh for longer, proper storage is essential. Once completely cooled, store the bread in a paper bag or a bread box at room temperature. Avoid using a plastic bag, as it can trap moisture and make the crust soft. Sourdough bread is best consumed within the first few days. If you have more bread than you can consume, consider freezing the extra loaves. Slice the bread before freezing, and place parchment paper between the slices to prevent them from sticking together. Frozen sourdough bread can be thawed at room temperature or lightly toasted before serving.

Tip: When storing sourdough bread, it's best to use a paper bag or a bread box rather than a plastic bag. Plastic can trap moisture and make the crust soft, while a paper bag or bread box allows the bread to breathe, maintaining its crustiness.

In conclusion, diving into the world of sourdough bread baking is an enriching and fulfilling experience. It offers not only delicious and wholesome loaves but also a deeper connection to the art and science of breadmaking. Throughout the process, you've learned to cultivate a healthy and robust sourdough starter, honed your skills in mixing, shaping, and scoring, and developed an understanding of the importance of time, temperature, and fermentation.

As you continue to practice and experiment with different techniques and variations, you'll discover your own signature loaf—unique in flavor, texture, and appearance. Remember that every loaf you bake tells a story, from the moment you mix the ingredients to the final golden crust.

Sourdough baking is a journey that intertwines tradition and creativity. It's a journey that connects you to a rich history of breadmaking, dating back centuries. Embrace the occasional challenges and setbacks as opportunities to learn and grow, for even the most experienced bakers continually refine their craft.

So, keep your starter alive, keep your oven hot, and keep your passion for sourdough bread alive. Enjoy the process, share your creations with loved ones, and take pride in the fact that you've mastered the art of sourdough bread baking. May your loaves be crusty, your crumb tender, and your enjoyment abundant. Happy baking!

Chapter 4
Breakfast Goodies

Sausage and Sourdough Bread Strata

Prep time: 10 minutes | Cook time: 20 minutes | Makes 8 to 12 squares

Indulge in the delightful flavors of Sausage and Sourdough Bread Strata, a dish that effortlessly marries comfort and elegance. This recipe is perfect for those cozy weekend brunches or for hosting a gathering of dear friends and family.

The beauty of this strata lies in its layers of flavors and textures. The tangy sourdough bread harmonizes splendidly with the savory goodness of sausage, creating a symphony of taste that will leave your taste buds dancing. The creamy custard mixture soaks into the bread, resulting in a luscious, melt-in-your-mouth experience.

For a complete breakfast or brunch experience, pair this Sausage and Sourdough Bread Strata with a simple green salad dressed in a light vinaigrette. The freshness of the salad will provide a lovely contrast to the richness of the strata. Additionally, consider serving it alongside a refreshing fruit platter to add a touch of natural sweetness to the meal.

When preparing this dish, it is crucial to allow sufficient time for the strata to rest and set. This ensures that the custard mixture fully absorbs into the bread, resulting in a moist and tender texture. Be sure to follow the recommended baking time and resist the temptation to rush this step.

So, gather your loved ones around the table and treat them to the irresistible allure of Sausage and Sourdough Bread Strata. Its warm, comforting aroma and exquisite flavors will make it an instant favorite, leaving everyone eager to savor each delightful bite. Get ready to embark on a culinary journey that is sure to create lasting memories.

- 4 cups sourdough bread, cubed
- 1 lb. breakfast sausage or italian sausage, cooked and crumbled
- 2 cups sharp cheddar cheese, shredded (if you buy a block of cheese and shred it yourself, the cheese is meltier)
- 12 eggs
- 2¼ cups milk
- 2 tsp. dry ground mustard
- 1 tsp. salt
- ½ tsp. ground pepper

1. Assemble the strata the night before so you can bake it in the morning. This recipe uses sourdough bread and is great for using up leftover bread.

THE NIGHT BEFORE:

1. Grease or butter a 9 × 13-inch baking dish. Mix the bread cubes and cooked sausage and spread evenly across the bottom of the pan. Next, sprinkle the shredded cheese evenly over the top of the sausage and bread.
2. In a medium mixing bowl, beat together the eggs, milk, dry mustard, salt, and pepper until thoroughly combined. Pour the egg mixture over the bread cubes, sausage, and cheese. Cover the baking dish with aluminum foil, crimping the edges for a snug fit. Refrigerate overnight.

THE NEXT DAY:

3. Remove the strata from the refrigerator, leave it covered, and set it on the counter to warm up a bit (about 30 minutes).
4. Preheat the oven to 350°. Bake the strata for 30 minutes, still covered with the aluminum foil; remove the foil and continue baking for 25 to 30 more minutes or until the strata is puffed and the middle is set. Cut it into squares and serve.

Sourdough Bread French Toast

Prep time: 10 minutes | Cook time: 20 minutes | Makes 8 slices

Transport yourself to a realm of breakfast bliss with the heavenly creation that is Sourdough Bread French Toast. This recipe presents a delightful twist on a classic morning favorite, perfect for leisurely weekend mornings or when you crave a touch of nostalgia.

What sets this Sourdough Bread French Toast apart is the extraordinary depth of flavor imparted by the tangy sourdough bread. The slight sourness of the bread complements the sweet custard bath, resulting in a harmonious balance that will tantalize your taste buds. The bread's rustic crust provides a delightful contrast to the tender, custard-soaked interior, adding an extra layer of textural bliss.

To elevate your Sourdough Bread French Toast experience, consider serving it with a medley of fresh berries, a dusting of powdered sugar, and a drizzle of pure maple syrup. The vibrant burst of fruity sweetness perfectly complements the rich and indulgent flavors of the French toast, creating a symphony of taste.

To achieve the perfect texture and flavor, it is essential to use day-old sourdough bread. This allows the bread to absorb the custard mixture without becoming too soggy. Additionally, make sure to preheat your griddle or skillet properly to ensure a golden brown and evenly cooked French toast.

Embark on a breakfast adventure as you savor each golden bite of Sourdough Bread French Toast. With its delightful flavor profile and enchanting aroma, this dish is bound to become a beloved addition to your breakfast repertoire. So, ignite your senses and relish the simple pleasure of a classic dish reinvented.

- 4 eggs
- ½ cup milk
- salt and pepper to taste
- 8 thick slices sourdough bread
- butter for cooking

1. In a flat-bottomed dish such as a glass pie plate or baking dish, beat together the eggs, milk, and salt and pepper until well mixed. (You can also use a blender to mix the ingredients.) Add the slices of sourdough bread and let them soak up the egg mixture.
2. Melt some butter in a skillet or griddle over medium heat; add the soaked slices of bread and cook for several minutes or until the bottom is golden brown; flip the French toast and cook the second side until done and golden brown. Be careful to watch the temperature so the French toast doesn't burn or get too dark before cooked through.
3. Serve plain or with butter, powdered sugar, or maple syrup.

Milk and Basil Bread

Prep time: 10 minutes | Cook time: 2 hours | Makes 1 loaf

Introducing our delightful Milk and Basil Bread, a unique fusion of flavors that will transport your taste buds to new realms of culinary satisfaction. With a harmonious combination of almond milk and fresh basil, this bread showcases the perfect balance between richness and herbaceousness.

Our recipe was carefully crafted to cater to those seeking a bread that marries wholesome ingredients with exceptional taste. The almond milk lends a subtle nutty undertone, while the aromatic basil infuses each slice with a refreshing herbal essence. The result is a bread that is both comforting and captivating, making it a standout choice for any occasion.

Whether you're planning a leisurely brunch or a cozy evening meal, our Milk and Basil Bread offers versatility that will enhance any dining experience. Toast it to perfection and savor it on its own, spreading a thin layer of butter for a simple yet satisfying treat. Alternatively, elevate your culinary creations by using this bread as a foundation for delightful sandwiches, pairing it with your favorite fillings such as roasted vegetables, savory meats, or creamy spreads.

During the production process, it's crucial to ensure the almond milk is incorporated smoothly with the sugar and other ingredients. The bread machine, set to the white bread setting and medium crust, will work its magic, allowing the dough to rise and develop its distinct flavors. Patience is key, as the bread requires time to cool down after baking, ensuring optimal texture and flavor development.

The Milk and Basil Bread is a true testament to the beauty of homemade bread, and it serves as a wonderful expression of your culinary prowess. Its aroma will fill your kitchen with a tantalizing fragrance, and its taste will leave a lasting impression on your palate. Share this bread with loved ones, and watch as their faces light up with delight.

Experience the delightful combination of almond milk and basil in our Milk and Basil Bread, and discover a whole new world of flavors and textures. Let it become a staple in your kitchen, providing moments of joy and satisfaction with every slice. Embrace the art of breadmaking and savor the magic that unfolds within your home.

- 1 cup almond milk
- 1 tablespoon sugar
- 1 tablespoon basil, chopped
- 3 tablespoons butter, soft
- 3 cups bread flour
- 1 teaspoon salt
- 2 teaspoons dry machine yeast

1. In the bread machine, mix the milk with the sugar and the other ingredients, chose the white bread setting and medium crust and start the machine.
2. Cool down and serve.

Cream Cheese Biscuits

Prep time: 10 minutes | Cook time: 40 minutes | Makes 12 biscuits

Indulge in the delectable allure of Cream Cheese Biscuits, a heavenly creation that will leave you yearning for more. With their flaky and buttery texture, these biscuits are a delightful addition to any meal or a perfect treat on their own.

The secret to the irresistible appeal of these Cream Cheese Biscuits lies in the combination of cream cheese and butter. These two ingredients, when frozen and incorporated into the dough, create pockets of rich and creamy goodness within each biscuit. The addition of sourdough discard adds a subtle tang, enhancing the overall flavor profile.

These Cream Cheese Biscuits shine when served warm, accompanied by a generous slathering of soft butter and a dollop of your favorite jam. The contrasting textures and flavors of the creamy butter and sweet jam beautifully complement the flaky, savory biscuits. Enjoy them as a delightful breakfast treat or as a delightful accompaniment to soups, stews, or roasted meats.

For the best results, ensure that the cream cheese and butter are thoroughly frozen before incorporating them into the dough. This step is essential as it helps create those desirable pockets of creamy goodness within the biscuits. Additionally, make sure to freeze the cut biscuits briefly before baking to help them hold their shape and rise beautifully.

Prepare to be enchanted as the aroma of freshly baked Cream Cheese Biscuits fills your kitchen. The golden-brown exterior and tender, flaky interior will captivate your senses and leave you craving another bite. Whether enjoyed on their own or as part of a memorable meal, these biscuits are sure to become a cherished addition to your culinary repertoire.

- 56 g (4 tbsp) cream cheese
- 114 g (½ cup) unsalted butter
- 56 g (¼ cup) sourdough discard
- 170 g (¾ cup) whole milk
- 25 g (5 tsp) cornstarch
- 300 g (2½ cups) all-purpose flour
- 14 g (1 tbsp) granulated sugar
- 14 g (4 tsp) baking powder
- 4 g (½ tsp) salt
- 3 g (½ tsp) baking soda
- 180 g (¾ cup) cream

1. About 30 minutes to 1 hour before you are ready to bake, cut the cream cheese and butter into ½-inch (1.3-cm) pieces and put them in the freezer.
2. Place a rack in the middle of your oven and preheat it to 450°F (230°C). Line a 9 x 13-inch (23 x 33-cm) baking sheet with parchment paper.
3. In a large measuring cup, combine the sourdough discard and milk. Put it in the refrigerator until you're ready to use it.
4. In a large mixing bowl, whisk together the cornstarch, flour, sugar, baking powder, salt and baking soda until no lumps remain. Add the frozen cream cheese and butter pieces into the flour mixture, using a pastry blender to cut both into the flour until the mixture resembles coarse crumbs. Stir in the cold milk mixture. Your dough should look dry and shaggy.
5. Turn your dough out onto a work surface and knead briefly until the dough comes together. Roll the dough into an 8-inch (20-cm) square, cut it into four equal squares and stack the pieces. Using a rolling pin, flatten the stack into an 8 x 6-inch (80 x 15-cm) rectangle. Trim the edges and cut the dough into 12 squares of roughly the same size. Place the squares on your prepared baking sheet and freeze for 5 to 10 minutes.
6. Remove the pan from the freezer and brush the tops of the biscuits liberally with cream. Bake them until they are light brown, about 12 to 15 minutes. Transfer the biscuits to a wire rack and let them cool for 5 minutes. Serve warm, with a generous slathering of soft butter and jam.
7. Store unbaked biscuits by freezing them uncovered on a baking sheet for 2 hours and then transferring them into a ziptop bag. Do not thaw frozen biscuits before baking. Bake according to the directions above, but you may have to add 3 to 5 minutes to the baking time.

Toad in the Hole

Prep time: 10 minutes | Cook time: 20 minutes | Serves 6

Indulge in the classic comfort of Toad in the Hole, a dish that brings together the simplicity of bread and eggs to create a satisfying and wholesome meal. Perfect for a leisurely breakfast or a delightful brunch gathering, this recipe is sure to please all who partake.

Toad in the Hole is a versatile dish that suits various occasions. Its quick and straightforward preparation makes it ideal for those busy mornings when time is of the essence. It is equally fitting for relaxed weekend brunches, where friends and family can gather around the table to savor its rustic charm.

The magic of Toad in the Hole lies in the delightful combination of buttery toasted bread and perfectly cooked eggs. The buttered sourdough bread adds a delightful crunch, while the eggs nestled in the middle provide a creamy and rich indulgence. The contrasting textures and flavors create a harmony that is both comforting and satisfying.

To enhance the experience of Toad in the Hole, consider serving it alongside a fresh garden salad or roasted vegetables. The crispness of the greens or the earthy flavors of the vegetables provide a lovely contrast to the warm and comforting elements of the dish. Add a sprinkle of salt and pepper to the eggs or allow your guests to season them according to their preference at the table.

When preparing Toad in the Hole, take care to ensure that the skillet is preheated adequately before adding the bread slices. This will result in a golden and evenly toasted crust. Additionally, when cracking the eggs into the bread holes, handle them gently to avoid breaking the yolks prematurely.

Allow yourself to relish the simple pleasure of Toad in the Hole—a delightful combination of toasted bread and eggs that transcends time and fills your kitchen with an irresistible aroma. Share it with loved ones, and watch as their faces light up with joy and satisfaction. May this cherished recipe become a staple in your culinary repertoire, bringing comfort and happiness to your table whenever it is served.

- butter for spreading, room temperature
- 6 slices thick-sliced sourdough bread with a hole cut or torn out of the middle, about 4 inches in diameter (or use a biscuit cutter)
- 6 eggs
- salt and pepper to taste

1. Spread butter on both sides of the bread slices.
2. Set the bread on a preheated skillet. Cook on medium-low heat until the undersides are golden brown and toasted. Turn the bread over and crack an egg into the hole of each piece of bread. Sprinkle with salt and pepper if desired (or salt and pepper them at the table when serving). Cover the skillet and cook until the egg whites are set. If desired, you can quickly flip the pieces of toast over to the first side to cook the eggs a bit firmer.

White Country Bread

Prep time: 10 minutes | Cook time: 2 hours | Makes 1 loaf

Immerse yourself in the delightful aroma and taste of freshly baked White Country Bread, a classic staple that embodies the essence of comfort and tradition. This recipe invites you to embark on a journey of bread-making mastery, resulting in a loaf that boasts a golden crust and a tender crumb.

White Country Bread is a versatile bread that can be enjoyed in a multitude of scenarios. Its simplicity and versatility make it a perfect choice for everyday sandwiches, whether it's a hearty turkey club or a simple ham and cheese. It can also be a charming addition to a rustic brunch spread or a delightful accompaniment to a comforting soup or stew.

The beauty of White Country Bread lies in its straightforward yet masterful combination of ingredients. The blend of white flour and bread flour creates a texture that is both soft and chewy. The addition of olive oil adds a subtle richness, while the yeast and baking powder work together to give the loaf a delightful rise and a tender crumb.

White Country Bread is wonderfully versatile when it comes to pairing. Enjoy it simply with a slather of creamy butter or transform it into a delectable sandwich filled with your favorite ingredients. It also serves as an excellent companion to soups, stews, and hearty dips, as it soaks up flavors and adds a delightful element of satisfaction to every bite.

When using a bread machine for this recipe, it is important to follow the machine's instructions and set it to the appropriate settings. Ensure that the yeast is fresh and active to ensure proper rising. After the bread is baked, allow it to cool before slicing to achieve the best texture and flavor.

Delight in the mastery of bread-making as you savor each slice of homemade White Country Bread. Let its golden crust and pillowy interior transport you to a world of comfort and nostalgia. Whether enjoyed as part of a meal or simply as a warm slice with a cup of tea, this bread is a testament to the joy that comes from creating something wholesome and delicious.

- 2 and ½ cups white flour
- 1 and ½ cups water
- 1 cup bread flour
- 1 teaspoon baking powder
- 2 and ½ teaspoons bread machine yeast
- 2 teaspoons sugar
- 1 tablespoon olive oil
- 1 teaspoon salt

1. In the bread machine, mix the flour with bread flour, water and the other ingredients, set the machine on quick setting and medium crust.
2. Push the start button and cool the bread down before serving.

Whole Bread

Prep time: 10 minutes | Cook time: 2 hours | Makes 1 loaf

Introducing our Whole Bread, a masterpiece of nourishment and flavor that will satisfy your cravings for a robust and wholesome loaf. With meticulous attention to detail, we have combined the finest ingredients to create a bread that embodies both satisfaction and nutrition.

This recipe caters to those seeking a bread that goes beyond mere sustenance. Bursting with the goodness of whole wheat flour, coconut milk, and a touch of brown sugar, our Whole Bread embraces the essence of wholesomeness and natural flavors.

Ideal for various occasions, this bread caters to the needs of individuals looking to incorporate more whole grains into their diet. Whether you desire a substantial foundation for sandwiches, a delightful accompaniment to breakfast, or a simple indulgence on its own, our Whole Bread delivers versatility to elevate your daily meals.

Crafted with the discerning palate in mind, our recipe takes advantage of the health benefits found in whole wheat flour, which boasts higher fiber and nutrient content compared to refined white flour. The addition of luscious coconut milk introduces a subtle richness, while the touch of brown sugar enhances the bread's inherent sweetness. These carefully selected ingredients work in harmony to create a symphony of flavors that will leave you yearning for more.

To fully experience the delightful possibilities, we recommend toasting a slice of our Whole Bread and lavishing it with your preferred nut butter or avocado for a satisfying and wholesome breakfast. The bread pairs exquisitely with savory fillings such as grilled vegetables, creamy hummus, or thinly sliced roasted turkey, making it a versatile foundation for mouthwatering sandwiches. Enhance your meal by accompanying it with a comforting bowl of homemade soup or a vibrant salad for a complete and nourishing feast.

During the production process, ensure the water is at the ideal temperature, allowing the yeast to work its magic without compromising its efficacy. By following the Whole Wheat mode on your bread machine, you create the optimal environment for the dough to rise and bake to perfection. Once baked, exercise patience and let the bread cool completely before slicing, ensuring each bite yields the finest texture and flavor.

Discover the wholesome delight of our Whole Bread, a culinary masterpiece that nourishes both body and soul. With its hearty texture, enticing aroma, and harmonious flavors, it will become an indispensable staple in your kitchen, bringing the joys of wholesome eating and the satisfaction of homemade bread to your table. Share the goodness with your loved ones, spreading the love for nourishing meals and the simple pleasures that come with them.

- 1 and ½ cups warm water
- 2 tablespoons avocado oil
- 1 teaspoon salt
- 1/3 cup brown sugar
- 3 tablespoons coconut milk
- 2 teaspoons dry yeast
- 4 and ½ cups whole wheat flour

1. In the bread machine, mix the water with the oil and the other ingredients.
2. Cook the bread using the Whole Wheat mode and cool the bread down before serving.

Apple Fritters

Prep time: 10 minutes | Cook time: 20 minutes | Makes about 20 small fritters or 12 large fritters

Apple Fritters are a delightful treat that can be enjoyed in various scenarios. Serve them as a special breakfast indulgence to start your day on a sweet note. They also make a delightful addition to brunch gatherings or as a homemade treat for family and friends. These fritters are perfect for those moments when you crave something comforting and utterly satisfying.

The magic of Apple Fritters lies in the combination of diced apples and the tangy notes of the starter. The apples provide a burst of fruity sweetness, while the starter adds depth and complexity to the flavor profile. The addition of cinnamon adds warmth and enhances the overall aroma, making each bite an irresistible delight.

Enjoy the Apple Fritters warm and freshly fried for the ultimate experience. If desired, sprinkle them with cinnamon sugar to add an extra layer of sweetness. Serve them as a delightful standalone treat, pair them with a steaming cup of coffee or tea, or even complement them with a dollop of whipped cream or a scoop of vanilla ice cream for a decadent dessert.

To achieve the best results, ensure that the diced apples are well coated with the starter, as this helps bind the fritters together during frying. It's essential to maintain the oil at the correct temperature of 360 to 370°F (182 to 188°C) to achieve a crisp and golden exterior. Be mindful not to overcrowd the skillet, allowing each fritter to have ample space for even frying.

Prepare to be enchanted by the heavenly aroma and delightful texture of Apple Fritters as they sizzle in the frying pan. Their golden-brown exterior, tender interior, and the burst of sweetness from the apples will captivate your taste buds with each delectable bite. Share these homemade delights with loved ones and create cherished moments filled with joy and indulgence.

- 3 cups diced apples, peeled or left with skins on
- 1 cup starter (discard is fine)
- ½ tsp. ground cinnamon
- ¼ tsp. salt
- ¼ tsp. baking soda
- oil for frying
- cinnamon sugar for sprinkling (optional)

1. Place the diced apples in a large mixing bowl. Slowly add the starter, mixing gently as you go, until combined. (You want the apple pieces well coated with starter, so you might need to add a bit more starter to achieve that—it helps to keep the fritters together when you fry them.)
2. Whisk together the cinnamon, salt, and baking soda and gently stir the mixture into the apples. Let the mixture rest while you heat the oil for frying.
3. Put about 2 inches of oil in a heavy cast-iron deep-sided skillet and heat to 360 to 370°. Drop the fritter batter into the hot oil, being careful not to crowd them. Fry for 2 to 3 minutes on each side or until golden brown. Use a slotted spoon to place the fritters on paper towels to drain. Sprinkle with cinnamon sugar if using and serve.

Lemon Ricotta Pancakes

Prep time: 10 minutes | Cook time: 40 minutes | Makes 8 pancakes

Indulge in the exquisite combination of tangy lemon and creamy ricotta with our delightful Lemon-Ricotta Pancakes. These pancakes are a delightful twist on the classic breakfast staple, offering a burst of citrus freshness and a tender, fluffy texture that will awaken your taste buds.

Lemon-Ricotta Pancakes are a delightful addition to any breakfast or brunch gathering. These pancakes are perfect for lazy weekend mornings when you have time to savor the flavors and enjoy a leisurely meal. They also make a delightful surprise for special occasions or when you simply want to treat yourself to a truly indulgent breakfast experience.

The beauty of Lemon-Ricotta Pancakes lies in the delicate balance of flavors. The sourdough discard adds depth and complexity, while the ricotta cheese provides a luxurious creaminess. The bright lemon zest and juice infuse the pancakes with a refreshing tang, elevating the overall taste. These pancakes are the epitome of comfort with a touch of elegance.

Serve Lemon-Ricotta Pancakes warm, fresh off the griddle, and generously drizzled with maple syrup. The natural sweetness of the syrup beautifully complements the tangy lemon and creamy ricotta. For an extra burst of freshness and color, top the pancakes with a handful of fresh berries, such as blueberries or raspberries. The vibrant berries add a delightful pop of flavor and create a visually stunning presentation.

When preparing the batter, be mindful not to overmix, as this can result in rubbery pancakes. Gently stir the ingredients until they are just combined, leaving a few lumps in the batter. This will ensure light and fluffy pancakes. When cooking the pancakes, melt butter on the skillet to create a sizzling base that adds a golden crust to each pancake.

Allow yourself to be transported to a realm of flavor and texture with each bite of our Lemon-Ricotta Pancakes. Let the bright citrus notes dance on your palate as you savor the velvety richness of the ricotta. With every fluffy pancake, you'll discover a delightful balance of tanginess, creaminess, and sweetness. Share these delectable creations with loved ones, and create memories that will linger long after the last pancake has been devoured.

- 113 g (½ cup) sourdough discard
- 28 g (2 tbsp) granulated sugar
- 88 g (½ cup) full-fat ricotta cheese
- 56 g (¼ cup) whole milk
- 1 large egg
- zest of 1 lemon
- 21 g (2 tbsp) fresh lemon juice
- 7 g (1 tsp) vanilla extract
- 60 g (½ cup) all-purpose flour
- 4 g (¾ tsp) baking soda
- ⅓ tsp baking powder
- ⅓ tsp kosher salt
- butter
- Suggested Toppings:
- maple syrup
- fresh berries

1. In a large bowl, mix the sourdough discard, sugar, ricotta, milk, egg, lemon zest, lemon juice and vanilla until they're combined. Sift the flour, baking soda, baking powder and salt into the bowl, and stir gently with a wooden spoon until only a few lumps remain. Avoid over-mixing the batter or your pancakes will turn out rubbery.
2. Heat a medium skillet over medium heat. Melt 14 grams (1 tablespoon) of butter on the skillet and wait for it to sizzle. Pour ¼ cup (60 ml) of the batter onto the skillet to make about a 5-inch (13-cm) pancake. Cook until it's golden brown, about 1 to 2 minutes on each side.
3. These pancakes are best served warm with maple syrup and fresh berries. Freeze leftover pancakes in a ziptop bag and toss them in the microwave for 40 seconds to reheat.

Mint Bread

Prep time: 10 minutes | Cook time: 2 hours | Makes 1 loaf

Welcome to the refreshing world of Mint Bread, where the aromatic essence of mint leaves comes together with the warm embrace of freshly baked bread. This delightful recipe offers a unique twist to traditional bread, infusing it with the invigorating flavors of mint for a truly memorable culinary experience.

Our carefully crafted Mint Bread recipe combines the perfect balance of ingredients to create a loaf that is both fragrant and flavorful. The addition of chopped mint leaves brings a refreshing herbal note, elevating the taste profile of the bread to new heights. With each bite, you'll be greeted by the cool and invigorating essence of mint, creating a delightful sensation on your palate.

Versatility is a key characteristic of our Mint Bread, allowing it to shine in a variety of settings. Enjoy it as a standalone treat, where the subtle sweetness from honey and the delicate aroma of mint take center stage. Alternatively, use it as a foundation for creative sandwiches, pairing it with complementary ingredients such as fresh vegetables, savory meats, or even creamy spreads.

Preparing Mint Bread is a breeze with the assistance of a bread machine. Simply combine warm water, freshly chopped mint, and the remaining ingredients, allowing the machine to work its magic. Select the white bread setting and medium crust for optimal results, and let the tantalizing aroma of mint fill your kitchen as the dough rises and bakes to perfection.

After the baking process is complete, allow the Mint Bread to cool before indulging in its irresistible flavors. The cooling period ensures that the bread achieves the ideal texture and allows the mint-infused flavors to fully develop. Serve it as a centerpiece of your meal or share it with loved ones, creating moments of joy and satisfaction with each slice.

Experience the invigorating and delightful combination of mint and bread with our Mint Bread recipe. Let its unique flavors transport you to a place of freshness and culinary excellence. Whether enjoyed as a breakfast staple, a satisfying snack, or a complement to your favorite dishes, this bread is sure to leave a lasting impression on your taste buds.

Embrace the opportunity to infuse your baking repertoire with the invigorating flavors of mint, and watch as your culinary creations take on a whole new dimension. Indulge in the wonders of Mint Bread and savor the magic that unfolds with every bite.

- 1 cup warm water
- 1 tablespoon mint, chopped
- 3 tablespoons honey
- 3 tablespoons coconut oil, melted
- 3 and ½ cups white flour
- 1 teaspoon salt
- 2 teaspoons dry machine yeast

1. In the bread machine, mix the warm water with mint and the other ingredients, select the white bread setting and medium crust and start the machine.
2. Cool down and serve.

Blackberry-Ginger Scones

Prep time: 10 minutes | Cook time: 40 minutes | Makes 8 scones

Blackberry-Ginger Scones are a delightful addition to any morning tea, brunch gathering, or a leisurely breakfast at home. Their elegant flavor profile and visually enticing appearance make them a perfect choice for special occasions or when you want to impress your guests with a homemade treat. These scones also make a delightful gift for friends and loved ones.

The beauty of Blackberry-Ginger Scones lies in the contrast of flavors. The juicy blackberries provide a burst of natural sweetness, while the grated fresh ginger adds a delightful warmth and complexity. The sourdough discard, yogurt, and milk contribute to the scones' tender crumb and moist texture, creating a truly delightful eating experience.

Enjoy these delectable scones while they are still warm from the oven, allowing the blackberries to release their sweet juices and the ginger to infuse every bite. Serve them with a dollop of clotted cream or your favorite fruit preserves for an extra touch of indulgence. Pair them with a fragrant cup of tea or freshly brewed coffee to create a delightful morning ritual or afternoon tea experience.

To ensure the best results, handle the dough with care and avoid overworking it. Incorporate the dry ingredients gradually, being careful not to overmix the dough, as this can result in tough scones. When cutting the scones into wedges, use a sharp knife or a bench scraper to maintain clean edges. Chilling the scones before baking helps them retain their shape and ensures a flaky texture.

Experience the sublime pleasure of each bite as you savor the tender crumb, juicy bursts of blackberries, and the subtle heat of ginger in our Blackberry-Ginger Scones. Allow yourself to be transported to a realm of refined flavors and delicate textures. Share these delightful treats with loved ones, creating cherished moments filled with warmth and culinary delight.

- 113 g (½ cup) sourdough discard
- 1 large egg
- 150 g (⅔ cup) yogurt, sour cream or crème fraiche
- 75 g (⅓ cup) whole milk, plus more for brushing
- 50 g (¼ cup) granulated sugar
- 7 g (2 tsp) baking powder
- 2 g (½ tsp) baking soda
- 3 g (½ tsp) salt
- 4 g (2 tbsp) grated fresh ginger
- 300 g (2½ cups) all-purpose flour
- 114 g (½ cup) unsalted butter, cold, cut into pieces
- 130 g (1 cup) fresh blackberries

1. In a large measuring cup, stir together the sourdough discard, egg, yogurt and milk until everything is fully incorporated. Put the mixture in the refrigerator until you're ready to use it.
2. In a large bowl, whisk together the sugar, baking powder, baking soda, salt, ginger and flour. Add the butter and toss to coat. Using a pastry blender, cut the butter into the flour until only pea-sized pieces remain. Lightly toss the blackberries in the flour mixture. Form a well in the middle of the flour and pour the cold milk mixture into the center. Using a fork, incorporate the dry ingredients gradually, until a shaggy dough forms (it's okay if the dough appears dry). Lightly knead the dough in the bowl until it just comes together. Do not overwork or your scones will become tough.
3. Line a 9 x 13-inch (23 x 33-cm) baking sheet with parchment paper. Turn your dough out onto a lightly floured surface and pat it into a round disk about 1 inch (2.5 cm) thick. Cut the dough into eight wedges and place them on the lined baking sheet about 2 inches (5 cm) apart. Put the scones in the refrigerator for 30 minutes.
4. While your scones chill, preheat the oven to 375°F (190 °C).
5. Brush the tops of the scones with milk and bake until they're golden brown, about 25 to 30 minutes. Move them to a wire rack and cool slightly before serving. These scones are best enjoyed fresh but will keep well in an airtight container for up to 2 days.

Chapter 5
Classic Sourdough Breads

Caramelized Onion Bread

Prep time: 10 minutes | Cook time: 20 minutes | Makes 1 loaf

Welcome to the delightful world of Caramelized Onion Bread! This recipe combines the irresistible aroma and flavor of sweet, golden-brown onions with a fluffy, homemade bread that will leave you craving for more. As a professional and kind chef, I'm excited to guide you through this culinary adventure, providing you with insights into the recipe's applicable scenarios, special analysis, matching suggestions, and production process precautions.

Caramelized onions are a culinary gem that adds a rich and savory touch to any dish. In this recipe, we take the time to slow-cook the onions to perfection, allowing their natural sweetness to develop and infuse the bread with incredible depth of flavor. The process of caramelization creates a harmonious balance between sweetness and umami, elevating the taste profile of this bread to new heights.

This Caramelized Onion Bread is perfect for various occasions. Its warm and comforting aroma makes it an ideal choice for cozy family gatherings or brunches with friends. Served fresh from the oven, it can be enjoyed as a standalone treat or paired with a variety of spreads, cheeses, or charcuterie. The sweet and savory combination of caramelized onions offers a delightful contrast that will tantalize your taste buds.

When preparing this recipe, it's crucial to pay attention to the caramelization process of the onions. Cooking them slowly and gently ensures they develop a rich, golden color without burning. Take care to stir them regularly, adding a touch of oil if needed to prevent sticking. The caramelized onions can be prepared in advance and refrigerated until you're ready to incorporate them into the dough.

As you embark on creating this delectable bread, follow the step-by-step instructions with precision. The dough, enriched with the caramelized onions, undergoes a series of resting and folding sessions to develop its texture and flavor. Patience is key during the rising stages, allowing the dough to double in size and develop a light and airy crumb. Remember to slash the top of the loaf before baking to allow for controlled expansion in the oven.

So, tie your apron, gather your ingredients, and let's dive into the world of Caramelized Onion Bread. Get ready to savor every bite of this savory, aromatic delight that will impress your guests and create lasting culinary memories. Enjoy the journey and the rewarding outcome of your efforts as you indulge in a slice of this homemade masterpiece.

- Caramelized Onions:
- 1 t. olive oil (a bit more if needed)
- ½ large onion, chopped into small pieces
- ¼ tsp. granulated sugar
- ¼ tsp. salt
- Bread Dough:
- 533 g. unbleached all-purpose flour
- 267 g. active starter
- 267 g. water
- 13 g. salt
- caramelized onions from the recipe above

1. In a medium skillet, heat the oil on medium heat. Add the onion and stir to coat the pieces with oil. Add the sugar and salt and cook, stirring so the onion pieces don't burn, until the onions have softened and turned a light golden brown (about 20 minutes). If the onions seem to get dry, you can add a small amount of oil to keep them from sticking to the pan and burning. When done, transfer the caramelized onions to a small container and refrigerate them until needed.
2. In a large bowl, combine all the ingredients except the salt and caramelized onions. Cover the bowl with plastic wrap and let the dough sit at room temperature for about 30 minutes. Sprinkle the salt throughout the dough and mix well again to fully incorporate the salt. Keeping the dough in the container, stretch and fold the dough 3 times, covering the bowl with plastic wrap and letting the dough rest for 30 minutes between sessions each time. After the third stretch and fold session, cover the dough and allow it to rest for 30 minutes. Then add the caramelized onions, kneading gently to begin mixing the pieces throughout the dough. Perform 3 more stretch and folds 30 minutes apart, covering the bowl between sessions.
3. Keeping the bowl covered with plastic wrap, let the dough rise until about doubled, usually 4 to 8 hours or overnight.
4. Gently turn the dough out onto a floured work surface and shape it. Cover with plastic wrap and let rise for about 4 hours or until almost doubled.
5. Slash the top. Preheat the oven to 400 to 450° and bake for 45 to 50 minutes or until done.

Cheesy Jalapeño Bread

Prep time: 10 minutes | Cook time: 20 minutes | Makes 1 loaf

This bread is a delightful fusion of tangy cheddar cheese, fiery jalapeño peppers, and a fluffy, homemade dough. It's perfect for those who crave a hint of spice and a burst of cheesy goodness in every bite. The contrasting flavors and textures make this bread an excellent choice for gatherings, picnics, or simply indulging in a delicious homemade treat.

Before we dive into the recipe, we need to prepare a starter the night before. This allows the flavors to develop and provides the bread with a light and airy texture. The starter is a crucial component, adding depth and complexity to the final loaf.

In the morning, we combine the starter with water and flour, working the dough until it becomes smooth and elastic. This dough undergoes a series of stretch and fold sessions, which develop the gluten and create structure. Adding the jalapeño peppers and sharp cheddar cheese brings a burst of flavor and a delightful hint of heat to every slice.

Proper shaping and scoring are essential to ensure an attractive loaf and controlled expansion during baking. Preheating the oven and using a Dutch oven or baking stone create the perfect environment for a crusty exterior and a soft, tender interior.

During the baking process, the tantalizing aroma of cheese and jalapeño peppers fills your kitchen, building anticipation for the moment you can savor a slice of this Cheesy Jalapeño Bread. Remember to allow the loaf to cool on a wire rack before slicing to preserve its texture and flavors.

Whether you're hosting a casual get-together, looking for an exciting addition to your bread basket, or simply craving a flavor-packed snack, this Cheesy Jalapeño Bread is sure to please. It pairs wonderfully with soups, stews, or even enjoyed on its own with a dollop of butter. Get ready to embrace the delightful combination of cheese and spice in a homemade loaf that will leave you craving more.

STARTER:

- 1/4 cup (50g) unbleached all-purpose flour
- 1/4 cup (50g) water
- 1/2 tablespoon (15g) starter

BREAD DOUGH:

- Starter made the night before
- 1 1/2 cups (360g) water
- 4 1/4 cups (500g) unbleached all-purpose flour, or a combination of whole wheat and all-purpose flours
- 2 teaspoons (10g) salt
- 1/4 cup (50g) sliced jalapeño peppers (fresh, roasted, or pickled)
- 1 cup (100g) sharp cheddar cheese, shredded

THE NIGHT BEFORE:

1. In the large mixing bowl you plan to make the bread dough in, mix the starter ingredients; cover with plastic wrap and let the starter sit at room temperature overnight.

THE NEXT MORNING:

1. In the bowl that contains the prepared starter, add the water and stir to combine. Whisk the flour and salt together and add to the starter, mixing with your hands and working until there are no dry bits of flour. (I like to mix in about half the flour mixture with a large spoon and then add the remaining flour mixture and mix by hand.) Cover the bowl with plastic wrap and let the dough rest at room temperature for 2 hours.
2. Perform 2 sets of stretch and folds 30 minutes apart, and cover the bowl when the dough is resting. After the second stretch, fold, and rest period, add the jalapeño peppers and cheese and stretch and fold 3 to 4 more times at 30-minute intervals, covering the bowl each time. After the last stretch and fold, cover the bowl and let the dough rise for 2 to 3 hours.
3. Turn the dough out onto a floured work surface and shape the dough into a circle or oblong. Flour the outside of the dough, cover it, and let it rise at room temperature for about 3 hours.
4. Preheat the oven to 450°. If using a Dutch oven or similar bread baker, place the baking dish into the oven to also preheat.
5. Slash the top of the loaf with a razor or lame and then carefully place the loaf into the preheated Dutch oven. (I use the lid for my base and the Dutch oven itself for the cover as it's much easier to get the loaf situated.)
6. Bake covered for 30 minutes; remove the top and continue baking for an additional 20 to 25 minutes. If using a baking stone or sheet, place a pan of boiling water in the oven on a rack under the bread to add steam to the baking. Remove the bread from the Dutch oven and set it on a wire rack to cool before slicing.

Sunflower Seed Bread

Prep time: 10 minutes | Cook time: 20 minutes | Makes 1 loaf

Welcome to the world of Sunflower Seed Bread! This recipe combines the wholesome goodness of sunflower seeds with the comforting aroma of freshly baked bread. With its nutty flavor and soft, chewy texture, this bread is a delightful addition to any meal or a satisfying snack on its own.

Designed for those seeking a hearty and nutritious option, this recipe showcases the richness of whole wheat flour and the unique touch of durum flour. The inclusion of sunflower seeds adds a delightful crunch and a subtle nuttiness, elevating the overall taste experience. Whether you enjoy it toasted with a spread of butter or as a foundation for your favorite sandwich, this bread is sure to please your palate and nourish your body.

To ensure the perfect outcome, it's important to give attention to the details. Preparing the starter the night before allows the flavors to develop and the dough to rise to its full potential. The gentle resting and rising periods the next morning contribute to the bread's structure and optimal texture.

Once you've shaped the dough, it's time for the magic to happen in the oven. As the aromas fill your kitchen, rest assured that the golden crust and tender crumb are on their way. Be patient as you await the final result, and allow the bread to cool on a wire rack to preserve its freshness.

Sunflower Seed Bread is a versatile creation, suitable for various occasions. From breakfast toast to sandwich bread for a picnic, it adapts to your culinary desires. Get ready to savor each bite, enjoying the delightful blend of flavors and the nourishing benefits it offers.

So, roll up your sleeves, gather your ingredients, and embark on a baking adventure that will yield a delightful loaf of Sunflower Seed Bread, destined to bring joy to your table.

- 1 cup (240 g) active starter
- 1 tsp butter
- 1 cup (240 g) milk
- 1/2 cup raw sunflower seeds
- 1 tsp honey
- 1 tsp salt
- 1 1/4 cups (175 g) whole wheat flour
- 1 cup + 2 tbsp (140 g) durum flour (you can substitute half whole wheat and half all-purpose flour)
- 1 1/4 cups (175 g) all-purpose flour

1. Pour the starter into a large mixing bowl and set aside for now.

THE NIGHT BEFORE:

1. In a microwaveable bowl, melt the butter and then add the milk; stir in the sunflower seeds, honey, and salt. Check the temperature of the butter and milk mixture to make sure it's no warmer than 100°. When cool enough, add this mixture to the large mixing bowl that contains the starter and combine well. Add the whole wheat flour and durum and mix by hand. Start adding the all-purpose flour a bit at a time, mixing after each addition. When the dough becomes too stiff to mix by hand, turn out the dough onto a floured work surface and knead in the remaining flour. Continue kneading the dough until it's smooth and satiny (about 8 minutes). Cover the bowl with plastic wrap and let the dough sit at room temperature overnight to double in bulk.

THE NEXT MORNING:

1. Gently turn out the dough onto a floured work surface and allow the dough to rest for 30 minutes. Shape the dough into the shape you want. Place the loaf onto a baking sheet or into a loaf pan and let it rise at room temperature for 2 to 4 hours, or however long you need for the loaf to about double in size (if a loaf pan is used, let it rise to the top of the loaf pan).
2. Place the pan into a cool oven and then turn the oven to 375°. Bake for 65 to 70 minutes. Remove the bread from the oven (and loaf pan if using) and place it on a wire rack to cool.

Almond Blackberries Bread

Prep time: 10 minutes | Cook time: 1 hour | Makes 1 loaf

Indulge in the delightful flavors of Almond Blackberry Bread, a treat that combines the richness of almond flour with the vibrant burst of fresh blackberries. This recipe brings together the nutty essence of almonds, the subtle sweetness of brown sugar, and the enticing aroma of vanilla extract, creating a bread that will captivate your taste buds.

To begin, gather the ingredients and prepare to embark on a baking adventure. Almond flour takes the spotlight, providing a delicate yet robust base for this bread. Chopped almonds add a delightful crunch, adding texture and enhancing the almond's natural flavors. The combination of almond flour and chopped almonds forms a harmonious blend that will leave you craving more.

Incorporate the remaining ingredients, including brown sugar, baking powder, active yeast, eggs, melted butter, and vanilla extract, into the mixture. These elements work together to create a smooth and cohesive dough, ensuring a tender and moist final product.

Once the dough is thoroughly mixed, transfer it to a loaf pan that has been generously coated with cooking spray. This step guarantees easy release and a beautifully shaped loaf. Allow the bread to bake in a preheated oven at 400 degrees Fahrenheit, filling your kitchen with the enticing aroma of toasty almonds and sweet blackberries. As the bread bakes, the flavors meld together, and the loaf transforms into a golden masterpiece.

After patiently waiting for the bread to bake for approximately one hour, remove it from the oven and allow it to cool. The anticipation builds as the scent fills the air, promising a delightful treat that awaits your enjoyment. Once cooled, carefully slice the bread into thick, luscious pieces that reveal the vibrant specks of mashed blackberries throughout.

Almond Blackberry Bread is best savored on its own or accompanied by your favorite spreads and toppings. From a simple slather of butter to a dollop of creamy almond butter or a drizzle of honey, this bread pairs wonderfully with various flavor combinations. Allow your taste buds to explore the delightful balance of nuttiness and fruity sweetness in each bite.

Whether enjoyed as a breakfast delight or an afternoon treat, Almond Blackberry Bread is a delightful addition to any occasion. Its enticing aroma, nutty flavors, and juicy bursts of blackberries create a sensory experience that will leave you longing for more. Share this homemade bread with loved ones or savor it as a moment of personal indulgence. Let the magic of almonds and blackberries come together in this delectable bread, offering a tantalizing escape to a world of delightful flavors.

- 2 cups almond flour
- 2 tablespoons almonds, chopped
- ½ cup brown sugar
- 2 teaspoons baking powder
- 1 teaspoon active yeast
- 2 eggs, whisked
- 1 and ½ cups almond flour
- ¼ cup butter, melted
- 1 tablespoon vanilla extract
- 1 cup blackberries, mashed
- cooking spray

1. In a bowl, mix the flour with the baking powder, yeast and the other ingredients, stir until you obtain a smooth dough, pour it into a loaf pan greased with cooking spray.
2. Bake at 400 degrees F for 1 hour, cool down, slice and serve.

Walnut Bread

Prep time: 10 minutes | Cook time: 20 minutes | Makes 1 loaf

Indulge in the rich, earthy flavors of Walnut Bread, where the wholesome combination of whole wheat and all-purpose flours meets the delightful crunch of walnut pieces. This recipe presents a harmonious blend of textures and flavors, creating a bread that is both satisfying and nutritious.

Crafted with care, this recipe begins by combining the flours, walnut pieces, and salt, resulting in a foundation that celebrates the natural goodness of walnuts. The addition of active starter infuses the bread with complexity and depth, while a touch of walnut oil (optional) enhances the nutty aroma and enriches the overall experience.

The process of stretching and folding the dough at regular intervals allows for the development of a robust gluten structure, ensuring a light and airy crumb. Patience is rewarded as the dough rises, doubling in size to create a bread with a delightful height and appealing appearance.

As the aroma of freshly baked walnut bread fills your kitchen, you'll be eager to savor each slice. The golden crust, adorned with signature slashes, gives way to a tender crumb, speckled with the goodness of walnuts. Enjoy a warm slice with a slather of butter or create a delectable sandwich filled with your favorite ingredients.

When it comes to baking, every detail counts. Preheating the oven to the suggested temperature allows for optimal browning and a perfect bake. As the bread emerges from the oven, transfer it to a wire rack to cool, preserving its texture and ensuring a delightful eating experience.

Walnut Bread is a versatile choice, suitable for a cozy breakfast, a hearty lunch, or a satisfying snack. Its nutty flavor pairs well with both sweet and savory accompaniments, offering endless possibilities to delight your taste buds.

So, embark on a culinary adventure, allowing the aroma of freshly baked Walnut Bread to fill your home. With its enticing flavors, nourishing ingredients, and artisanal charm, this bread is sure to become a favorite in your kitchen.

- 1 1/2 cups (200 g) unbleached all-purpose flour
- 1 1/2 cups (200 g) whole wheat flour
- 1/3 cup (40 g) walnut pieces
- 2 tsp (10 g) salt
- 1 cup + 2 tbsp (265 g) water
- 1 cup (200 g) active starter
- 1 tsp walnut oil (optional)

1. In a medium mixing bowl, stir together the flours, walnut pieces, and salt. Add the remaining ingredients, mix to combine, and then let the dough sit for about 30 minutes. Keeping the dough in the container, stretch and fold the dough every 30 minutes or so about 6 times. Cover the bowl and let the dough rise until about doubled, usually 4 to 8 hours or overnight.
2. Gently turn out the dough onto a floured work surface and shape it. Cover and let rise for about 4 hours or until about doubled.
3. Slash the top. Preheat the oven to 400 to 450° and bake for 40 to 50 minutes or until done. Cool on a wire rack.

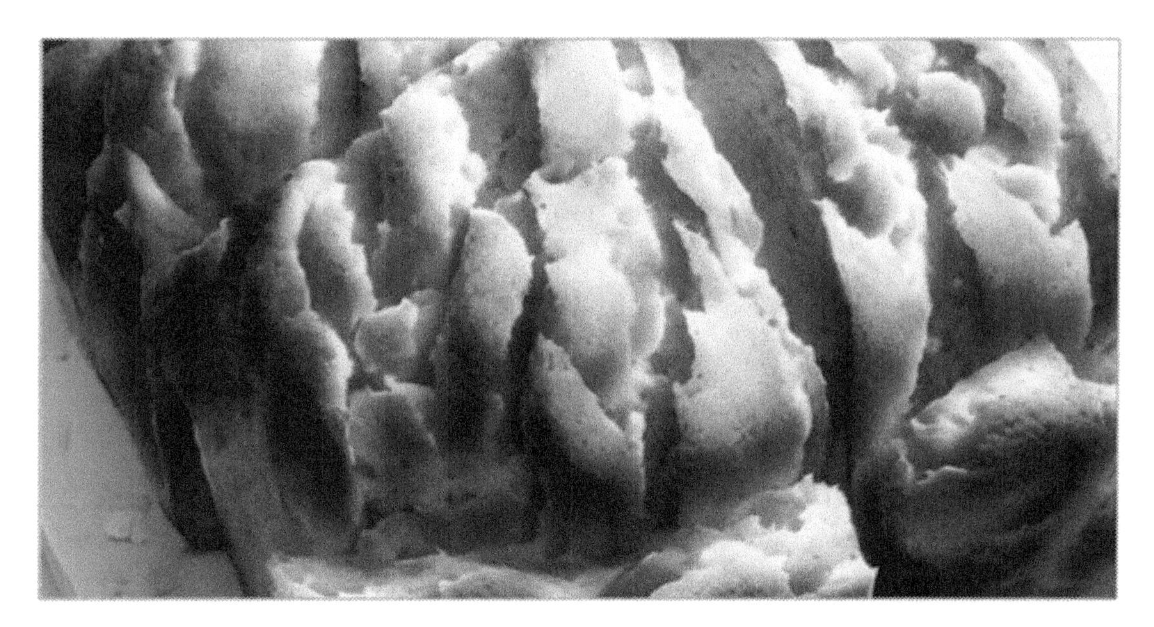

Whole Wheat Bread

Prep time: 10 minutes | Cook time: 20 minutes | Makes 1 loaf

Experience the hearty goodness of Whole Wheat Bread, a classic recipe that celebrates the natural richness of whole wheat flour. With its robust flavor and nourishing qualities, this bread is a comforting staple that will delight your senses and satisfy your cravings.

Crafted with simplicity, this recipe calls for a handful of ingredients that come together harmoniously. Whole wheat flour takes center stage, offering a nutty and slightly sweet taste profile, while the addition of water and starter creates a lively and flavorful dough. These wholesome elements combine to form a bread that embodies rustic charm and wholesome goodness.

The process begins by gently mixing the ingredients, allowing the dough to rest and develop its structure. Patience is key as the dough rises, doubling in size to create a loaf with an inviting height and a satisfying texture. Throughout the rising process, regular stretching and folding of the dough enhance its structure, resulting in a light and airy crumb.

As the aroma of freshly baked whole wheat bread fills your kitchen, anticipation builds for that first warm slice. The crust, adorned with signature slashes, develops a beautiful golden hue, while the interior showcases a tender and flavorful crumb. Whether enjoyed simply with a spread of butter or used as the foundation for sandwiches and toasts, each bite of this homemade bread is a celebration of wholesome flavors.

To achieve optimal results, preheating the oven to the suggested temperature ensures a well-browned and evenly baked loaf. Once baked to perfection, transfer the bread to a wire rack to cool, preserving its texture and allowing flavors to settle.

Whole Wheat Bread is a versatile companion for various meals and occasions. From hearty sandwiches to morning toasts, this bread adds a wholesome touch to your everyday culinary adventures. Embrace the goodness of whole grains, and let this bread become a reliable presence on your dining table.

Experience the joy of creating your own homemade bread, as the aroma of freshly baked whole wheat bread permeates your home. With its robust flavor, nourishing ingredients, and satisfying texture, this recipe invites you to savor the simple pleasures of wholesome baking.

- 2 3/4 cups (400 g) whole wheat flour
- 1 cup + 2 tbsp (250 g) water
- 3/4 cup (200 g) starter
- 2 tsp (10 g) salt

1. In a large bowl, mix all the ingredients except the salt. Let the dough sit for about 45 minutes; sprinkle the salt over the dough and mix well again to fully incorporate the salt throughout. Keeping the dough in the container, stretch and fold the dough every 30 minutes or so about 6 times. Cover the bowl and let the dough rise until about doubled, usually 4 to 8 hours or overnight.
2. Gently turn out the dough onto a floured work surface and shape it. Cover and let rise for about 4 hours or until about doubled.
3. Slash the top. Preheat the oven to 400 to 450° and bake for 40 to 45 minutes or until done. Cool on a wire rack.

Vanilla Raspberries Bread

Prep time: 10 minutes | Cook time: 1 hour | Makes 1 loaf

Prepare to embark on a culinary journey that will captivate your senses and leave you craving more.
To begin, gather the ingredients and let your kitchen be filled with the tantalizing aroma of freshly baked bread. White flour forms the base, providing a light and fluffy texture that perfectly complements the fruity bursts of raspberries. Baking powder ensures a gentle rise, creating a tender crumb that melts in your mouth.
Add a touch of sweetness with erythritol, a natural sugar substitute that adds a subtle sweetness without the extra calories. Balancing the flavors, a hint of salt enhances the overall taste profile, bringing out the natural sweetness and adding depth to each bite.
Whisk the egg and combine it with almond milk, melted ghee, and vegetable oil. These ingredients work harmoniously to create a moist and flavorful bread, ensuring a delightful texture and a richness that will make each slice a true pleasure to enjoy. The addition of vanilla extract lends a heavenly aroma and a comforting warmth that complements the tartness of the raspberries.
Gently fold in the vibrant raspberries, allowing their juicy goodness to infuse the bread with bursts of fruity sweetness. As the bread bakes, the raspberries soften and release their vibrant color, creating an enticing mosaic throughout the loaf.
Transfer the batter into a lined loaf pan, ensuring an even distribution. Allow the bread to bake in a preheated oven at 350 degrees Fahrenheit, filling your home with the delightful aroma of freshly baked goodness. As the bread rises and turns golden brown, anticipation builds for the moment you can sink your teeth into a slice.
After patiently waiting for approximately one hour, remove the bread from the oven and allow it to cool. The aroma that wafts through the kitchen is simply irresistible, promising a delightful treat that awaits your enjoyment. Once cooled, slice the bread into generous pieces, revealing the vibrant red hues of the raspberries scattered throughout.

Vanilla Raspberry Bread is a versatile delight that can be enjoyed on its own or paired with your favorite spreads. From a simple smear of butter to a dollop of creamy cream cheese or a dusting of powdered sugar, the options are endless. Each bite offers a symphony of flavors, from the fragrant vanilla to the bursts of tart raspberries.
Whether enjoyed as a morning treat, an afternoon pick-me-up, or a sweet dessert, Vanilla Raspberry Bread is a delightful addition to any occasion. Its harmonious blend of flavors and moist texture make it a crowd-pleaser for family gatherings, brunches, or simply as a moment of personal indulgence. Share the joy by serving this homemade bread to loved ones or savor it as a well-deserved treat for yourself. Let the enchanting combination of vanilla and raspberries transport you to a world of sweet satisfaction with every delicious bite.

- 2 cups white flour
- 1 teaspoon baking powder
- ¾ cup erythritol
- ½ teaspoon salt
- 1 egg
- ¾ cup almond milk
- ¼ cup ghee, melted
- 2 cups raspberries
- 2 teaspoons vanilla extract
- ¼ cup vegetable oil

1. In a bowl, mix the flour with the baking powder, salt and all the other ingredients and stir.
2. Pour this into a lined loaf pan and bake at 350 degrees F for 1 hour.
3. Cool the bread down, slice and serve.

Chapter 6: Whole Grain Breads and Sandwich Breads Recipes

Flax Bread

Prep time: 10 minutes | Cook time: 45 minutes | Makes 1 bread

Flax Bread is a versatile and healthy option that caters to various dietary preferences, making it an excellent choice for those seeking a gluten-free, low-carb, or keto-friendly alternative.

Flaxseed, known for its abundant omega-3 fatty acids, dietary fiber, and lignans, takes the center stage in this recipe, offering a host of health benefits. Combined with the subtle sweetness of coconut flour and the binding properties of eggs, this bread delivers a wholesome and nourishing experience.

To begin, we mix the flaxseed meal and coconut flour, carefully incorporating the other dry ingredients such as baking powder, baking soda, and salt. Next, we add the essential wet ingredients: whisked eggs, warm water, and a touch of tangy apple cider vinegar. These elements come together to form a dough that will transform into a flavorful loaf.

Once the dough is mixed and kneaded to a smooth consistency, we transfer it to a loaf pan, allowing it to bake to golden perfection at 350 degrees Fahrenheit for approximately 40 minutes. The aroma of freshly baked bread will soon fill your kitchen, inviting anticipation and excitement.

After the baking process, it is crucial to let the Flax Bread cool before indulging in its delightful flavors. Sliced and served on its own, this bread offers a nutty and slightly earthy taste that pairs wonderfully with a variety of spreads, from creamy avocado to tangy hummus. For a more substantial meal, consider using it to create delicious sandwiches or as a base for toasts, embracing the versatility of this nutritious creation.

With its wholesome ingredients and straightforward preparation, Flax Bread provides a delightful option for those seeking a healthy, homemade bread alternative. So, embark on this culinary journey and savor the taste of nourishment with each bite of Flax Bread.

- 1 cup flaxseed meal
- 4 eggs, whisked
- 1 cup coconut flour
- 1 teaspoon baking powder
- 1 teaspoon baking soda
- 1 teaspoon salt
- 1 tablespoon apple cider vinegar
- ½ cup warm water

1. In a bowl, mix the coconut flour with flaxseed meal and the other ingredients except the eggs and the water and stir.
2. Add the water and eggs, stir and knead until you obtain a dough.
3. Transfer it to a loaf pan and bake at 350 degrees F for 40 minutes before cooling and serving.

Spinach Corn Bread

Prep time: 10 minutes | Cook time: 40 minutes | Makes 2 loaves

Welcome to the world of delightful bread-making! Today, I bring you a recipe that combines the vibrant flavors of spinach and corn, resulting in a truly irresistible treat: Spinach Corn Bread. This recipe is perfect for those looking to add a nutritious twist to their bread while savoring a unique combination of ingredients.

With just a handful of pantry staples and a dash of creativity, you can create two wholesome loaves of Spinach Corn Bread that will captivate your taste buds. The preparation time of 10 minutes ensures a quick and convenient baking experience, making it ideal for busy individuals seeking a homemade bread that doesn't compromise on flavor.

This bread is a wonderful option for various occasions. Its vibrant green color and distinct flavor make it an excellent addition to your brunch table or a delightful accompaniment to a comforting soup or stew. The versatility of this recipe allows it to shine as a standalone snack or as part of a larger meal.

The combination of corn flour, spinach, and cheddar cheese in this recipe provides a delightful balance of textures and flavors. The corn flour brings a pleasant sweetness and a slightly crumbly texture, while the spinach adds a vibrant and nutritious element. The touch of cheddar cheese adds a subtle tang and a hint of indulgence.

When preparing this Spinach Corn Bread, it is important to ensure that the dough is well-mixed to achieve an elastic consistency. This will contribute to the bread's light and fluffy texture. Be sure to divide the dough equally between two loaf pans to ensure even baking and a beautiful golden crust.

Once out of the oven, allow the loaves to cool slightly before slicing. The aroma of freshly baked bread will fill your kitchen, and you'll be eager to taste the delightful combination of flavors within. Whether enjoyed warm with a pat of butter or as a base for a gourmet sandwich, Spinach Corn Bread promises a memorable culinary experience.

So, let's embark on this baking adventure together and create a sensational bread that celebrates the harmonious marriage of spinach and corn. Get your aprons on, gather your ingredients, and let's dive into the recipe for Spinach Corn Bread.

- 1 tablespoon olive oil
- 1 teaspoon salt
- ½ cup spinach, chopped
- 3 cups corn flour
- 1 cup warm water
- 1 teaspoon baking soda
- 1 tablespoon sugar
- ½ cup cheddar, shredded

1. In a bowl, mix the flour with the baking soda, sugar and the other ingredients, and stir well until you obtain an elastic dough.
2. Transfer the dough to 2 loaf pans, bake at 390 degrees F for 40 minutes, cool down, slice and serve.

Whole-Wheat Sourdough Rolls

Prep time: 8 hours 10 minutes | Cook time: 8 hours 40 minutes | Makes 24 rolls

Indulge in the wholesome goodness of freshly baked Whole-Wheat Sourdough Rolls. These delightful rolls are the epitome of homemade comfort, featuring the rich flavors of whole-wheat flour, sourdough starter, and a touch of sweetness from pure maple syrup or honey. With a perfectly soft and chewy texture, these rolls are sure to become a favorite addition to your bread repertoire.

Crafting these delectable rolls requires some patience and dedication, but the results are well worth the effort. The recipe emphasizes the use of a sourdough starter, which adds depth of flavor and contributes to the rolls' light and airy crumb. The process begins with activating the starter, allowing it to ferment and develop its unique tangy character.

Once the starter is ready, the bread dough comes together with the assistance of a stand mixer or handheld electric mixer. The combination of whole-wheat flour, water, salt, butter, and maple syrup or honey creates a well-balanced dough that is both easy to work with and packed with nutrition. As you mix the ingredients, adjust the flour as needed to achieve a slightly sticky yet manageable consistency.

After an initial period of kneading, the dough is left to rest and rise, allowing the flavors to develop and the gluten to relax. The dough is then divided into 24 pieces and shaped into beautiful rolls. The rolling technique involves a circular motion, resulting in tightly formed balls with a smooth surface. These rolls are arranged in a buttered baking pan and given a final rise under a floured kitchen towel, allowing them to reach their full potential.

Before baking, the rolls are marked with an X using a bread lame or a sharp knife, giving them a charming appearance. As they bake in the oven, a wonderful aroma fills your kitchen, and anticipation builds for the moment when you can savor these freshly baked treats. After a golden brown color is achieved, the rolls are brushed with melted butter, adding a final touch of richness.

Whole-Wheat Sourdough Rolls are perfect for a variety of occasions. Serve them warm alongside a bowl of soup or stew for a comforting meal, or use them to create delicious sandwiches packed with your favorite fillings. These rolls also make an excellent accompaniment to brunch or holiday gatherings.

So, let the aroma of freshly baked bread fill your home as you embark on the journey of making Whole-Wheat Sourdough Rolls. The combination of whole-wheat goodness, the tang of the sourdough starter, and a touch of sweetness will surely delight your taste buds and bring joy to those who share in this homemade delight. Get ready to enjoy these warm, soft, and flavorful rolls straight from your oven.

TOOLS NEEDED:

- stand mixer, 9-by-13-inch baking pan, bread lame or very sharp knife
- For Activating The Starter:
- 2 tablespoons to 2.4 ounces (¼ cup) sourdough starter
- 2 ounces (¼ cup) lukewarm (90°f to 100°f) pure filtered or bottled water
- 2 ounces (½ cup) whole-wheat flour
- For The Bread Dough:
- 4¾ ounces (½ cup) active whole-wheat sourdough starter
- 18 ounces (2¼ cups) cool (60°f to 70°f) pure filtered or bottled water
- 1½ teaspoons fine sea salt
- 2 ounces (¼ cup) butter, at room temperature, divided, plus more for preparing the baking dish
- 3 ounces (¼ cup) pure maple syrup, or honey
- 24 ounces (6 cups) whole-wheat flour, plus more as needed

TO ACTIVATE THE STARTER:

1. At least 6 to 12 hours before making the dough, in a medium bowl, combine the starter, lukewarm water, and flour, completely incorporating the ingredients into the starter. Loosely cover and let sit on the counter until ready to use.

TO MAKE THE BREAD DOUGH:

1. Early in the morning, in the bowl of a stand mixer fitted with the paddle attachment, or in a large bowl and using a handheld electric mixer, combine the active starter, water, salt, 2 tablespoons of butter, the maple syrup, and whole-wheat flour. Mix on low speed until the ingredients are fully combined, adding more flour if the dough is too sticky, but not more than 4 ounces (1 cup, or 7 cups total).
2. Attach the dough hook and knead on low speed for at least 10 minutes, or 15 to 20 minutes by hand.
3. Cover the bowl with a piece of plastic wrap and let the dough rest for 6 hours.
4. Coat a 9-by-13-inch baking pan with butter. Evenly divide the dough into 24 pieces. Flour a breadboard or clean work surface and, on it, shape each piece into a ball with a slightly open hand, rolling the dough in a circular motion until you get a tight surface. Place the rolls in the prepared pan. Flour a kitchen towel and cover the rolls with it. Let rise for 2 hours.
5. Preheat the oven to 375°F.
6. Using a bread lame or very sharp knife, mark each roll with an X. Melt the remaining 2 tablespoons of butter.
7. Bake the rolls for 25 to 30 minutes, or until brown. Remove from the oven and brush the rolls with melted butter before serving.

Bean Whole Wheat Bread

Prep time: 10 minutes | Cook time: 30 minutes | Makes 2 loaves

Discover a unique twist on traditional bread with our Bean Whole Wheat Bread recipe. This delightful bread incorporates the heartiness of whole wheat flour and the wholesome goodness of mashed Cherokee beans, resulting in a bread that is not only delicious but also packed with protein and fiber. With its rustic texture and subtle hint of hot paprika, this bread is sure to be a delightful addition to your baking repertoire.

Creating this Bean Whole Wheat Bread is a straightforward process that begins by mixing together the dry ingredients—corn flour, baking soda, and salt. Then, the star of the recipe, mashed Cherokee beans, is added, bringing a unique flavor and velvety texture to the dough. To add a touch of warmth and complexity, a hint of hot paprika is incorporated, balancing the flavors.

In a separate bowl, whisk together the eggs, olive oil, and milk, creating a creamy and nourishing base for the bread. The wet ingredients are then combined with the dry ingredients, stirring and kneading until a cohesive dough forms. This step ensures that all the ingredients are thoroughly combined and the dough is properly developed.

Once the dough is ready, it is divided into two loaf pans, allowing the bread to bake evenly and develop a beautiful golden crust. The loaves are then baked in a preheated oven at 400 degrees F for approximately 30 minutes. As the bread bakes, your kitchen will be filled with the enticing aroma of freshly baked bread, making it hard to resist the anticipation of tasting the final result.

After baking, the loaves are allowed to cool slightly before being sliced and served. The Bean Whole Wheat Bread pairs exceptionally well with a variety of spreads, from creamy hummus to tangy goat cheese. It also makes a delicious base for sandwiches or toast, adding a unique and nutritious element to your meals.

Not only does this bread offer a delightful flavor and texture, but it also provides the nutritional benefits of whole wheat flour and protein-packed Cherokee beans. It is a wonderful option for individuals seeking a bread recipe that incorporates plant-based ingredients and is suitable for vegetarian or vegan diets.

So, venture into the world of Bean Whole Wheat Bread and embrace the delightful combination of whole wheat goodness and the earthy flavors of mashed Cherokee beans. With its simple preparation and satisfying results, this bread is perfect for enjoying on its own or as a versatile canvas for your culinary creations. Bake a batch today and savor the deliciousness of homemade, bean-infused bread.

- 2 cups corn flour
- 1 teaspoon baking soda
- 1 teaspoon salt
- 2 cups canned Cherokee beans, drained, rinsed and mashed
- ½ teaspoon hot paprika
- 2 eggs, whisked
- 2 tablespoons olive oil
- 1 and ½ cups milk

1. In a bowl, mix the flour with baking soda, salt, beans and the other ingredients, stir and knead until you obtain a dough.
2. Divide this into 2 loaf pans, bake at 400 degrees F for 30 minutes, cool down, slice and serve.

Simple Sandwich Bread

Prep time: 2 hours and 40 minutes | Cook time: 40 minutes | Makes 1 loaf

Welcome to the world of homemade bread! Today, I'll be sharing with you a recipe for Simple Sandwich Bread. This classic loaf is the perfect staple for any kitchen, offering a soft and tender texture that is ideal for sandwiches, toasting, or simply enjoying on its own.

Whether you're a seasoned baker or just starting your bread-making journey, this Simple Sandwich Bread recipe is suitable for all skill levels. It's a great option for those looking to venture into the world of homemade bread, as it requires basic ingredients and straightforward techniques.

This recipe emphasizes simplicity without compromising on flavor and texture. The combination of all-purpose flour, milk, and hot water creates a light and airy crumb, while the addition of vegetable oil and sugar adds moisture and a touch of sweetness. The dry yeast provides the essential leavening power, ensuring a beautifully risen loaf.

The versatility of this Simple Sandwich Bread makes it a versatile addition to your kitchen. Slice it up to create delicious sandwiches with your favorite fillings, or toast it for a satisfying breakfast. You can also serve it alongside soups or stews, using it to soak up all the savory flavors.

When working with yeast, it's important to ensure that your ingredients are at the appropriate temperatures. Make sure the water is hot enough to activate the yeast but not too hot to kill it. Additionally, keep an eye on the rising times to ensure proper fermentation and a well-developed flavor.

Get ready to fill your home with the irresistible aroma of freshly baked bread as we embark on this journey to make Simple Sandwich Bread. Let's get started!

- 3 cups all purpose flour
- ½ cup milk
- 2/3 cup hot water
- 4 tablespoons vegetable oil
- 2 tablespoons sugar
- 1 tablespoon dry yeast
- ½ teaspoon salt

1. In a bowl, mix the flour with the yeast, water and the other ingredients, stir until you obtain a dough and transfer it to a floured working surface.
2. Knead the dough for 10 minutes, transfer to a bowl, cover and leave aside to rise for 1 hour.
3. Transfer the dough to a loaf pan, cover and leave aside to rise for another 1 hour and 30 minutes.
4. Bake at 350 degrees F for 40 minutes.

Chard Sandwich Bread

Prep time: 20 minutes | Cook time: 1 hour | Makes 2 loaves

Prepare to elevate your bread-making game with our delightful Chard Sandwich Bread recipe. This unique twist on classic sandwich bread incorporates vibrant Swiss chard, creating a loaf that is not only delicious but also packed with nutritious goodness. Get ready to embark on a culinary adventure and enjoy the satisfaction of baking your very own homemade bread. Whether you're seeking a wholesome loaf to serve as the foundation for your favorite sandwiches or you're looking to impress your loved ones with a special treat, Chard Sandwich Bread is the perfect choice. This recipe allows you to explore new flavors while maintaining the comfort and versatility of traditional sandwich bread.

By combining the earthy flavors of Swiss chard with a blend of eggs, olive oil, coconut oil, and melted butter, this bread achieves a rich and moist texture that will keep you coming back for more. The addition of cane sugar and stevia adds a touch of sweetness without overpowering the flavors. Meanwhile, the combination of white flour, baking soda, and instant yeast ensures a fluffy and well-risen loaf.

Chard Sandwich Bread pairs beautifully with a variety of fillings and spreads. Try using it to create gourmet sandwiches with fresh vegetables, deli meats, and flavorful cheeses. You can also enjoy it on its own, toasted and lightly buttered for a simple and satisfying snack. This bread also complements soups, salads, and charcuterie boards, adding a unique twist to your meal presentations.

When incorporating the Swiss chard into the dough, make sure it is thoroughly chopped to ensure even distribution throughout the bread. Additionally, when kneading the dough, pay attention to its consistency. If it feels too sticky, gradually add small amounts of flour until it becomes more manageable. Properly greasing and lining the loaf pans with parchment paper will help prevent sticking and ensure easy removal after baking. Get ready to experience the delightful flavors and vibrant colors of Chard Sandwich Bread. Let's dive into the recipe and enjoy the process of creating homemade bread that will impress both your taste buds and your loved ones.

- 5 Swiss chard leaves, chopped
- 3 eggs, whisked
- ¼ cup olive oil
- 1 cup cane sugar
- ½ cup stevia
- ¼ cup coconut oil, melted
- ¼ cup melted butter
- 1 teaspoon salt
- 3 cups white flour
- 1 teaspoon baking soda
- 1 teaspoon instant yeast

1. In a bowl, mix the yeast with flour, baking soda, salt and sugar, stir and leave aside for 10 minutes.
2. Add the rest of the ingredients, stir until you obtain a dough and knead for 10 minutes more.
3. Divide into 2 loaf pans lined with parchment paper and bake at 350 degrees F for 1 hour.
4. Cool down and serve.

Multi-Seed Sandwich Loaf

Prep time: 10 minutes | Cook time: 1 hour 35 minutes | Serves 4

Multi-Seed Sandwich Loaf - a delightful bread that combines the wholesome goodness of various seeds with a soft and flavorful crumb. This recipe is perfect for those who appreciate a hearty, nutrient-packed loaf that adds a delicious twist to your everyday sandwiches. With a prep time of just 10 minutes, this bread is incredibly convenient to make. The key to its exceptional taste and texture lies in the inclusion of a lively active starter, which infuses the loaf with a tangy undertone. The combination of golden flaxseeds, poppy seeds, millet seeds, sunflower seeds, and pumpkin seeds adds a delightful crunch and a burst of flavors to each bite. The use of strong white bread flour ensures a sturdy structure and a chewy texture that holds up well to sandwich fillings.

The production process for this loaf involves several rounds of pulls and folds, allowing the dough to develop strength and structure. The overnight fermentation at a cool room temperature further enhances the flavor complexity and yields a beautifully risen dough.

The Multi-Seed Sandwich Loaf offers great versatility. Its nutty and slightly sweet profile pairs wonderfully with various fillings, from classic deli meats and cheeses to fresh vegetables and spreads. The combination of seeds not only adds texture but also contributes to the overall nutritional value of the bread, making it a wholesome option for those seeking a balanced diet.

Whether you choose to preheat your oven or opt for a cold start, this loaf bakes to perfection in about 1 hour and 35 minutes. The aroma that fills your kitchen as it bakes is simply irresistible. To ensure doneness, tap the base of the loaf - a hollow sound indicates it's ready.

Once baked, allow the Multi-Seed Sandwich Loaf to cool on a wire rack for optimal slicing. This bread can be enjoyed fresh, toasted, or even used to make flavorful grilled sandwiches. Its long shelf life and versatility make it an excellent choice for batch baking and meal planning.

Elevate your sandwich game with this delightful Multi-Seed Sandwich Loaf. Its wholesome ingredients, delightful crunch, and exceptional taste will make every bite a truly satisfying experience.

- 50 g (¼ cup) active starter
- 375 g (1¾ cups) water
- 500 g (4 cups) strong white bread flour
- 25 g (⅛ cup) golden flaxseeds
- 25 g (⅛ cup) poppy seeds
- 25 g (⅛ cup) millet seeds
- 25 g (⅛ cup) sunflower seeds
- 25 g (⅛ cup) pumpkin seeds
- 7 g (1 tsp) salt, or to taste

1. In the early evening, in a large mixing bowl, roughly mix together all the ingredients until you have a shaggy, sticky dough with no bits of dry flour. Cover the bowl with a clean shower cap or your choice of cover and leave the bowl on the counter for 2 hours.
2. After 2 hours, perform the first set of pulls and folds, lifting and pulling the dough up and over itself in the bowl; the dough will be stiff from the seeds but easy to stretch. Stop when it comes into a soft ball. Cover the bowl again and leave it on your counter for 1 more hour.
3. After the hour, do another set of pulls and folds. The dough will be stretchier but still stiff and will easily come into a ball. Cover the bowl again.
4. Leave the covered bowl on the counter overnight, typically 8 to 10 hours, at 64 to 68°F (18 to 20°C).
5. In the morning, the dough will have grown to double in size. Have your pan ready and place the paper liner on the counter. Gently lift and fold small handfuls of dough from one side of the bowl into the middle in a line, using the same pulling and folding action as used previously. Turn the bowl 180 degrees and do the same on the other side so that you have a thick sausage of dough in the middle of the bowl.
6. With a wetted hand, place your whole hand over the dough, turn the bowl upside down and gently ease the dough from the bowl into your hand. Place the dough, seam side down, on the paper and slip your hand out from underneath the dough. Use the paper to lift the dough into the pan, cover it with the same shower cap and leave it on the counter.
7. Allow the dough to proof again, letting it grow level with the edge of the pan. This may take 2 to 3 hours, depending on the temperature of your kitchen. The surface will become smooth and the dough will spread to fill the pan. This step can also be done in the fridge for a longer, slower second proof—up to 24 hours—and can then be baked directly from the fridge.
8. Top Tip: You can follow my seed mix or create your own; you will need 125 g (½ cup plus 2 tbsp) of seeds in total.
9. This loaf can also be made using the same process as the Easy Shape Crusty White Loaf, using a round or oval banneton and baked in your bread pan.
10. When you are ready to bake, decide whether you would like to bake in a preheated oven or from a cold start. If preheating, set the oven to 350°F (180°C) convection or 400°F (200°C) conventional.
11. If you preheated the oven, put the lid on the pan and bake it for 45 minutes. If you are using a cold start, place the covered pan of dough in the oven, set the temperature as above and set a timer for 50 minutes.
12. Remove the bread from the oven and the pan, tap the base of the loaf and if it sounds hollow, the loaf is baked. If not, return it to the oven, out of the pan, directly onto the rack to bake it for a further 5 to 10 minutes. Remove it from the oven and allow it to cool on a wire rack for at least an hour before slicing.

Chapter 7
Pastry and Specialty Bread

Sourdough Donuts with Cinnamon Sugar

Prep time: 1 hour | Cook time: 20 minutes | Serves 1

Indulge in the delectable delight of homemade Sourdough Donuts with Cinnamon Sugar. These fluffy and flavorful treats are a true testament to the magic of sourdough. With a preparation time of just 1 hour and a cook time of 20 minutes, this recipe allows you to savor the satisfaction of freshly made donuts in no time.

The journey begins by combining warm whole milk, melted butter, egg, and active sourdough starter in a mixing bowl. Infused with the sweetness of granulated sugar and the aromatic blend of ground cardamom and cinnamon, this batter becomes the foundation of irresistible donuts. As you gradually incorporate the flour, the dough takes shape, transforming from sticky to smooth through the gentle kneading process.

After a period of rest, the dough undergoes a series of folds, further enhancing its texture and allowing the yeast to work its magic. Refrigerating the dough overnight intensifies the flavor and creates a dough that's ready to be shaped into delightful donuts.

On the following day, roll out the chilled dough to a thickness of 1/2 inch, resisting the urge to knead. Using round cutters, create perfectly shaped donuts and let them rise on oiled and lined baking sheets. The dough will gradually expand, and when a gentle indentation remains after pressing, it's a sign that they are ready to be fried.

In a large pot, heat the oil to 350 degrees Fahrenheit and fry the donuts in batches until they turn golden brown and puffed. With a satisfying crunch on the outside and a pillowy soft interior, these donuts are truly a delight to behold. As each donut emerges from the oil, roll it in a generous coating of cinnamon sugar, adding a sweet and aromatic touch to every bite.

For the ultimate enjoyment, savor these Sourdough Donuts with Cinnamon Sugar while they're still warm and fresh from the fryer. The combination of the tangy sourdough, fragrant spices, and sweet coating creates a harmonious symphony of flavors. Whether it's a weekend brunch, a special occasion, or a simple treat to brighten your day, these homemade donuts are sure to impress.

Note: Take caution while frying and handling hot oil. Ensure proper ventilation and follow safety guidelines to prevent accidents. Enjoy responsibly and savor the moment with every bite of these delightful donuts.

- 1 cup whole milk, warmed to about 120°F (slightly warmer than body temperature)
- 1 large egg (room temperature)
- ¼ cup unsalted butter, melted (½ stick)
- 1 cup active sourdough starter
- 4 cups unbleached all-purpose flour
- ½ cup granulated sugar
- 1 teaspoon ground cardamom
- 1 teaspoon ground cinnamon
- 1 teaspoon salt
- Cinnamon sugar for coating

PREPARE THE DOUGH (DAY 1):

1. Warm the milk, butter, and egg, then add them to a mixing bowl with the starter. Put in the sugar, spices, salt, and 300g of flour while the mixer is on. Make a thick batter by mixing for many minutes.
2. Put on the dough hook and incorporate the rest of the flour (the amount of flour may vary based on the hydration of your starter). To begin with, the dough will be pretty sticky. Knead on medium-low speed until the dough clings to the hook and clears the sides of the bowl, about 15 minutes (speed 2 on my stand mixer).
3. Dump the dough onto a floured board to knead it into a smooth ball. Put the dough in a bowl and turn it over once to coat it with the oil. Cover the dough and let it rest at room temperature for a few hours, allowing the yeast to work its magic.
4. After an hour, remove the dough from the bowl and fold it on one side. Repeat on the dough's other three sides, then flip it over. Keep the bowl covered and put it aside.
5. After the initial 2-3 hours of folding, you should continue the process once per hour. The dough should be energetic, elastic, and airy after 3-4 hours of fermentation. Give the dough an additional hour to rest at room temperature if it is still slowly rising. Refrigerate overnight if possible by covering and doing so.

DONUTS, PLEASE! (DAY 2):

1. Gather the dough and put it in a bowl. Roll the dough to a thickness of 1/2 inch on a lightly floured board while it is still cold, avoiding the temptation to knead.
2. Donuts may be easily shaped with a round cutter 4 inches in diameter. Put a hole in the middle with a 1.5" cutter. Space the doughnuts out on a baking sheet that has been oiled and lined with parchment paper or a silpat so that they have room to rise (I used 2 baking sheets). Apply a thin layer of oil to the doughnuts' surfaces. Donuts can be made indefinitely if you just keep rerolling the scraps and cutting them into shapes.
3. Place plastic wrap directly on the sheet pans in a warm, draft-free place to let the dough rise. Donuts are done when a dent is made in the dough with a finger, or a utensil slowly disappears. The dough isn't done if you press on it, and it bounces right back. There should be around a 1.5-hour delay in this ascent. The time required will change depending on the ambient temperature.
4. Meanwhile, bring 2 quarts of oil to 350 degrees Fahrenheit in a large, heavy pot. Fry the donuts in two or three batches for two to three minutes per side or until golden brown and puffed.
5. Roll each donut in cinnamon sugar as it comes out of the oil to ensure an even coating. While you fry the rest of the doughnuts, place these on a cooling rack.
6. Ideal consumption time is immediately after frying or when still warm.

Sourdough Danish Pastries

Prep time: 1 hours 15 minutes | Cook time: 15 minutes | Serves 1

Welcome to the world of Sourdough Danish Dough, where the tangy allure of sourdough meets the tender elegance of a classic Danish pastry. This recipe is a delightful exploration for those who revel in the intricate art of sourdough baking. The dough itself is a carefully orchestrated medley of flavors and textures, harmonizing active sourdough starter, sugar, kosher salt, ground cardamom, melted butter, eggs, milk, and pure vanilla extract. This symphony of ingredients yields a soft and buttery dough, infused with the enchanting essence of cardamom. The magic truly unfolds when the sourdough starter joins the dance, imparting a nuanced depth and inviting texture to every bite.

Navigating the production process requires both patience and precision. We will guide you through the steps, offering insights and recommendations to ensure your Danish pastries emerge flawlessly flaky and irresistible. Give the dough ample time to rise, allowing it to fully develop its characteristically tangy profile. Take care when crafting the dough, paying close attention to its texture and elasticity. The final shaping and baking stages hold the key to achieving the perfect golden hue and satisfyingly airy texture.

While the recipe features a delectable cheese filling, don't hesitate to embark on your own creative journey. Explore a myriad of sweet or savory fillings that speak to your palate's desires. Whether these pastries grace your breakfast table, enhance a delightful brunch, or dazzle guests at a special occasion, Sourdough Danish Dough promises a remarkable experience. So, channel your inner baker, embrace the allure of sourdough, and let these pastries transport you to a realm of culinary enchantment.

SOURDOUGH DANISH DOUGH:

- 7/8 cup (196g) active sourdough starter (100% hydration)
- 1/3 cup (70g) sugar
- 1 1/2 teaspoons (8g) kosher salt
- 1/2 teaspoon (2.5g) ground cardamom
- 1/4 cup (57g) unsalted butter, melted
- 1 large egg + 2 large egg yolks
- 3/4 cup + 2 tablespoons (184g) whole milk
- 1/2 teaspoon (2.5g) pure vanilla extract
- 4 1/2 cups (540g) unbleached all-purpose flour

BUTTER BLOCK:

- 1 cup (227g) unsalted butter, cold
- 1 tablespoon (8g) unbleached all-purpose flour

EGG WASH:

- 1 large egg
- 1 tablespoon (15g) milk

CHEESE DANISH FILLING FOR 16 PASTRIES:

- 8 ounces cream cheese, softened
- 1/4 cup (50g) powdered sugar
- 1 large egg yolk
- pinch of salt
- 1/2 teaspoon (2.5g) pure vanilla extract

GLAZE FOR 16 PASTRIES:

- 1 cup (125g) powdered sugar
- 2 tablespoons (31g) milk

DANISH SOURDOUGH:

1. The first step is to mix the sourdough starter, sugar, salt, cardamom, melted butter, egg, egg yolk, milk, and vanilla essence in a big basin. Stir in the flour using a Danish dough whisk or a spoon until a shaggy ball of dough forms.
2. The next step is to dump the dough onto a clean work surface and knead it for a few minutes or until it is smooth.
3. Set a ball with the dough in a bowl with the lid perched on top. Leave for 5 hours in a warm spot so the alcohol can develop. Cover and chill for 12 hours before serving (or up to 2 days).

A BLOCK OF BUTTER:

1. First, just before you're ready to laminate your dough on day two, make your butter block. Spread the flour on parchment paper and sprinkle the chilled butter on top.
2. Wrap the butter in the parchment paper loosely and use a rolling pin to flatten it until it becomes your desired thickness carefully.
3. Step 3: Fold the long sides of your 8 by 7-inch parchment paper over the butter and crease the edges (measure for accuracy).
4. making a rectangle of butter and parchment paper, 8 inches by 7 inches, by wrinkling the paper over the butter
5. You should next roll and push the butter to uniformly fill the rectangle.
6. Wrapped butter in a parchment paper block
7. If your butter has softened somewhat around the edges, place it in the fridge for a few minutes. For the next stage, the butter must be cold but very flexible and consistent with the dough.

BUTTER BLOCK LOCK:

1. First, get the dough out of the fridge and flatten it into a 16-by-10-inch rectangle with as even and square corners as you can manage.
2. Two put the butter block in the middle of the rectangle and fold the dough over it, so the ends meet in the middle of the butter. Use a pastry brush to remove any stray crumbs of flour.
3. Dough with a butter block in the middle, folded in on itself so that the butter is at the center.
4. It may be securely inserted by squeezing the butter block's edges together.
5. Third, join the central seam by pressing it together. Finally, seal the top and bottom borders by pressing them together to prevent the butter from leaking out as you roll.
6. The Book Fold, or Initial Fold
7. Turn the dough so the seam runs horizontally. 1. To make a rectangle, roll it out to 20 by 12 inches,

paying particular attention to the corners. If you want to flatten the dough uniformly before you roll it, gently pounding it with the rolling pin can assist.

8. Second, bring the two short sides of the rectangle together in the middle, and fold the rectangle in half lengthwise, book-style. Clean up any stray flour with a brush as you go.
9. The first fold is made by bringing the left side to the middle, and the second fold brings the right side to the middle.
10. The initial fold is accomplished by folding the dough in half, like a book, then sealing the two halves together.
11. Third, chill your dough in the fridge for 20 minutes in a plastic bag.
12. The Letter Fold, or the Second Fold
13. The first step is to uncover the dough from the refrigerator. Roll out the dough into a second rectangle, this time 20 by 12 inches, with the fold of the "book" horizontal to you.
14. The second step is to fold the dough in thirds like a letter.
15. View of dough from the side after the second fold, with the first edge folded in thirds and the second edge folded in half. Cover the dough with plastic wrap and refrigerate it overnight for at least an hour.
16. Prepare the Pastry:
17. Unwrap the dough. Cut the dough in half vertically from bottom to top with the folded side horizontal to you. Leave half of it out. Make a 16-by-8-inch rectangle with the remaining half.
18. After you've trimmed the dough with a pizza cutter, cut it into eight squares.
19. The trimmed dough is divided into 8 squares.
20. 2. Brush some egg wash over the center of one square. It's time to clinch the deal by folding the corners toward the center.
21. Bringing the four corners together and pushing
22. Step 3: Continue with the rest of the squares. Place pastries on half-sheet pans coated with parchment (no more than six per pan) and cover loosely with plastic wrap until ready to bake.
23. Repeat with the remaining dough, rolling, cutting, and shaping it as before (if you don't have enough baking sheets or oven space to bake more than one pan at a time, wrap the shaped pastries in plastic and refrigerate until ready to prove and bake).
24. After the dough has been made, it should be proofed in a warm environment until the pastries have risen and puffed.
25. Make the egg wash and cheese filling in parallel to step 6. In a little mixing bowl, thoroughly incorporate the egg and milk. I am putting aside. To make the cheese filling, soften the cream cheese and place it in a medium bowl. Beat in the remaining filling ingredients until combined. I am putting aside. To bake well, an oven temperature of 425 degrees Fahrenheit must be maintained.
26. After the pastries have been proofed, step seven is to wet your fingertips and press down on the middle of each one again to make room for the filling. Using an egg wash to coat the pastries lightly would be best.
27. use of egg wash for pastry
28. Eight, fill each with a spoonful of the cheese mixture. Then, sprinkle the cheese with about third as much preserves.
29. baked goods with filling
30. 9. Bake on the middle rack at 425 degrees Fahrenheit for 12-15 minutes or until golden brown, one pan at a time.
31. Make the glaze by blending the powdered sugar and milk in a blender or whisk. Use a plastic piping or zipper bag with the tip cut off to pipe glaze onto pastries, or pour it on with a fork.

Toasted Sunflower

Prep time: 5 minutes | Cook time: 15 minutes | Makes 1 loaf

Welcome to the world of Toasted Sunflower bread, where the warmth of homemade goodness and the delightful crunch of sunflower seeds come together in perfect harmony. This recipe is a testament to the art of bread-making, offering a simple yet satisfying loaf that will elevate any meal. With a blend of flours and the irresistible addition of toasted sunflower seeds, this bread promises a delightful sensory experience.

To create this masterpiece, you'll need an active starter, warm water, semolina flour, white whole wheat flour, white rye flour, bread flour, fine sea salt, and, of course, sunflower seeds. The production process involves a careful balance of mixing, shaping, rising, and baking to achieve the perfect texture and flavor.

As a versatile bread, Toasted Sunflower can find its place in various scenarios. Whether you're looking for a delicious addition to your breakfast table, a satisfying companion to your lunchtime sandwiches, or a delightful accompaniment to a cozy dinner, this loaf fits the bill. The nutty notes from the sunflower seeds add a distinctive touch, making it an ideal choice for those seeking a flavorful twist.

Throughout the production process, it's important to pay attention to details. From whisking the starter and water to incorporating the flours and shaping the dough, each step contributes to the final result. The scoring of the dough before baking allows for controlled expansion and a beautiful visual appeal. and when it comes to storing the loaf, keep it fresh in a plastic bag at room temperature for up to one day.

Savor the joy of baking your own Toasted Sunflower bread, and let the aroma and flavors fill your kitchen. With its rustic appearance and inviting texture, this bread will surely impress both family and guests. So, gather your ingredients, embark on this culinary adventure, and indulge in the simple pleasure of creating homemade bread that is sure to please all who taste it.

- 50 g (¼ cup) bubbly, active starter
- 365 g (1½ cups plus 1 tsp) warm water
- 100 g (⅔ cup) semolina flour
- 100 g (¾ cup plus 1 tbsp) white whole wheat flour
- 50 g (½ cup) white rye flour
- 300 g (2½ cups) bread flour
- 9 g (1½ tsp) fine sea salt
- 180 g (1½ cups) sunflower seeds, for coating

MAKE THE DOUGH:

1. In a large bowl, whisk the starter and water together with a fork. Add the flours and salt. Combine to form a rough dough, then finish mixing by hand until the flour is fully absorbed. Cover with a damp towel and let rest for 45 minutes to 1 hour. Meanwhile, replenish your starter with fresh flour and water, and store according to preference.
2. After the dough has rested, work it into a fairly smooth ball, about 15 to 20 seconds.

BULK RISE:

1. Cover the bowl with a damp towel and let rise at room temperature until double in size. This will take about 6 to 8 hours at 70°F (21°C). Optional Step: About 30 minutes into the bulk rise, stretch and fold the dough for added structure and height. Repeat this technique, about 2 to 3 sets, spaced 45 minutes apart (here).

SHAPE THE DOUGH AND COAT WITH SEEDS:

1. Remove the dough onto a floured work surface. Shape it into an oval and let rest for 5 to 10 minutes. Meanwhile, line a 10-inch (25-cm) oval proofing basket with a towel and set aside. Spread the sunflower seeds on a damp kitchen towel.
2. With floured hands, gently cup the dough and pull it toward you to tighten its shape. Lightly brush the surface and sides of the dough with water. Using a bench scraper, place the dough onto the seeds, wet side down. Lift both sides of the towel and rock it back and forth to coat the dough. Place the dough into your basket, seam side up.

SECOND RISE:

1. Cover the dough and let rest until puffy but not fully risen, about 30 minutes to 1 hour.
2. Preheat your oven to 450°F (230°C). Cut a sheet of parchment paper to fit the size of your baking pot.

SCORE:

1. Place the parchment over the dough and invert the basket to release. Score the dough straight down the length of the loaf, using the tip of a sharp paring knife or razor blade. Use the parchment to transfer the dough into the baking pot.

BAKE:

1. Bake the dough on the center rack for 20 minutes, covered. Remove the lid, and continue to bake for 40 minutes. When finished, transfer the loaf to a wire rack. Cool for 1 hour before slicing.
2. This loaf will stay fresh up to 1 day in a plastic bag, stored at room temperature.

Golden Sesame Semolina

Prep time: 5 minutes | Cook time: 15 minutes | Makes 1 loaf

Prepare to embark on a culinary journey with Golden Sesame Semolina bread, a delightful fusion of rich semolina flour and the irresistible nuttiness of sesame seeds. This recipe combines the artistry of bread-making with the enchanting flavors of the Mediterranean, resulting in a loaf that is as visually stunning as it is delicious. With a preparation time of just 5 minutes and a cook time of 15 minutes, you'll have a homemade bread that will leave a lasting impression. To create this masterpiece, you'll need a bubbling and active starter, warm water, semolina flour, bread flour, fine sea salt, and a generous amount of sesame seeds for the coating. The dough-making process involves a careful combination of mixing, shaping, rising, and baking, which all contribute to the texture and flavor profile of the final loaf.

Golden Sesame Semolina bread lends itself to a variety of scenarios. It is a perfect accompaniment to hearty soups and stews, an ideal base for open-faced sandwiches, and a wonderful addition to any mezze or charcuterie platter. The sesame seeds not only add a delightful crunch but also enhance the visual appeal of the bread, making it an elegant centerpiece for any table.

Throughout the production process, it's important to pay attention to detail. From whisking the starter and water to incorporating the flours and shaping the dough, each step plays a vital role. The scoring of the dough with a small serrated knife or razor blade allows for controlled expansion and adds an artistic touch to the loaf. To maximize freshness, store the bread in a plastic bag at room temperature for up to one day.

Indulge in the aroma and flavors of Golden Sesame Semolina bread, and allow your taste buds to transport you to the sun-kissed shores of the Mediterranean. This bread is a testament to the magic that can be created in your own kitchen. So gather your ingredients, follow the carefully crafted steps, and enjoy the satisfaction of creating a homemade bread that will impress family and friends alike.

- 50 g (¼ cup) bubbly, active starter
- 350 g (1⅓ cups plus 2 tbsp) warm water
- 250 g (1½ cups) semolina flour
- 275 g (about 2¼ cups) bread flour
- 9 g (1½ tsp) fine sea salt
- 120 g (¾ cup) sesame seeds, for coating

MAKE THE DOUGH:

1. In a large bowl, whisk the starter and water together with a fork. Add the flours and salt. Mix to combine, then finish by hand until the flour is fully absorbed. Cover with a damp towel and let rest for 45 minutes to 1 hour. Replenish your starter with fresh flour and water, and store according to preference.
2. After the dough has rested, work the mass into a fairly smooth ball, about 15 to 20 seconds. The dough will feel much softer at this stage.

BULK RISE:

1. Cover the bowl with a damp towel and let rise at room temperature, 70°F (21°C), until double in size, about 6 to 8 hours. Optional Step: About 30 minutes into the bulk rise, stretch and fold the dough for added structure and height. Repeat this technique, about 2 to 3 sets, spaced 45 minutes apart (here).

SHAPE THE DOUGH AND COAT WITH SEEDS:

1. Remove the dough onto a lightly floured work surface. Shape it into a round and let rest for 5 to 10 minutes. Meanwhile, line an 8-inch (20-cm) bowl or proofing basket with a towel. Spread the sesame seeds on a damp kitchen towel.
2. With floured hands, gently cup the dough and pull it toward you in a circular motion to tighten its shape. Then lightly brush the surface and sides of the dough with water. Using a bench scraper, place the dough onto the seeds, wet side down. Lift both sides of the towel and rock it back and forth to coat the dough. Place the dough into your bowl, seam side up.

SECOND RISE:

1. Cover the dough and let rest until puffy but not fully risen, about 30 minutes to 1 hour.
2. Preheat your oven to 450°F (230°C). Cut a sheet of parchment paper to fit the size of your baking pot.

SCORE:

1. Place the parchment over the dough and invert the bowl to release. Make three 4-inch (10-cm) long cuts in the shape of a triangle with a small serrated knife or a razor blade. Use the parchment to transfer the dough into the baking pot.

BAKE:

1. Bake the dough on the center rack for 20 minutes, covered. Remove the lid, and continue to bake for 40 minutes. Transfer the loaf to a wire rack and cool for 1 hour before slicing.
2. To maximize freshness, store at room temperature in a plastic bag, up to 1 day.

Rustic Pumpernickel

Prep time: 5 minutes | Cook time: 15 minutes | Makes 1 loaf

Welcome to the world of Rustic Pumpernickel, a bread that embraces the robust flavors of pumpernickel flour and the sweet depth of molasses. This recipe captures the essence of traditional bread-making, resulting in a loaf that is rustic in appearance and rich in taste. With just 5 minutes of preparation time and 15 minutes of cooking time, you'll have a homemade bread that will transport you to a cozy European bakery.

To create this masterpiece, you'll need a lively starter, warm water, unsulphured molasses, pumpernickel flour, bread flour, fine sea salt, oil, and optional fennel seeds for an extra burst of flavor. The dough-making process involves whisking the starter, water, and molasses together, adding the flours and salt, and kneading until a soft and pliable dough forms. A rest period allows the flavors to develop, and the addition of oil and fennel seeds brings an aromatic touch.

Rustic Pumpernickel is ideal for various occasions. It pairs beautifully with cured meats and cheese, making it a fantastic choice for charcuterie boards and sandwiches. Its robust flavor also complements hearty soups and stews, adding depth and character to every bite. With its unique appearance and complex taste, this bread is sure to impress both guests and family alike.

Throughout the production process, attention to detail is crucial. From whisking the starter and water to incorporating the flours and shaping the dough, each step contributes to the final result. The scoring of the dough before baking allows for controlled expansion and creates an attractive pattern on the loaf. It's important to monitor the browning of the bread during baking and tent with foil if needed to prevent over-browning.

Once baked to perfection, allow the Rustic Pumpernickel loaf to cool on a wire rack before slicing. To keep it fresh, store the bread in a plastic bag at room temperature for 1 to 2 days. This bread is best enjoyed within a couple of days, allowing you to savor its unique flavors and textures.

Indulge in the comforting aroma and wholesome taste of Rustic Pumpernickel, and transport yourself to the heart of European baking traditions. With its hearty character and distinct flavor profile, this bread is a testament to the artistry of bread-making. So gather your ingredients, follow the steps with care, and immerse yourself in the joy of creating homemade bread that embodies the rustic charm of old-world baking.

- 50 g (¼ cup) bubbly, active starter
- 365 g (1½ cups plus 1 tsp) warm water
- 40 g (2 tbsp) unsulphured molasses
- 120 g (1 cup) pumpernickel flour
- 380 g (about 3¼ cups) bread flour
- 9 g (1½ tsp) fine sea salt
- 30 g (2 tbsp) oil
- 5 g (1 tbsp) fennel seeds, optional

MAKE THE DOUGH:

1. In a large bowl, whisk the starter, water, and molasses together with a fork. Add the flours and salt. Combine until a thick, dense dough forms and then finish by hand until the flour is absorbed. Cover with a damp towel and let rest for 45 minutes to 1 hour. Meanwhile, replenish your starter with fresh flour and water, and store according to preference.
2. After the dough has rested, add the oil and fennel seeds, if using, to the bowl. Gently knead to incorporate or until the oil is well absorbed. The dough will feel much softer and not as stiff as it was earlier.

BULK RISE:

1. Cover the bowl with a damp towel and let rise at room temperature until double in size, about 8 to 10 hours at 70°F (21°C).

SHAPE:

1. Remove the dough out onto a lightly floured surface. Shape into a round and let rest for 5 to 10 minutes. Meanwhile, dust an 8-inch (20-cm) proofing basket with flour. With floured hands, gently cup the dough and pull it toward you in a circular motion to tighten its shape. Place the dough into your basket, seam side up.

SECOND RISE:

1. Cover the dough and let rest until puffy, but not double in size, about 1½ to 2 hours, depending on temperature.
2. Preheat your oven to 450°F (230°C). Cut a sheet of parchment paper to fit the size of your baking pot.

SCORE:

1. Place the parchment over the dough and invert the basket to release. Using the tip of a small knife or razor blade, make four shallow 4-inch (10-cm) long cuts at 3, 6, 9, and 12 o'clock around the dough. Then, make four leaf-shaped cuts in between. Use the parchment to transfer the dough into the baking pot.

BAKE:

1. Bake the dough, covered, on the center rack for 20 minutes. Remove the lid, and continue to bake for 40 minutes. If the loaf starts to brown too quickly because of the sugars in the molasses, loosely tent with foil. Transfer to a wire rack and cool for 1 hour before slicing
2. This sourdough will last for 1 to 2 days stored at room temperature in a plastic bag.

Fast Coconut and Cherry Tea Loaf

Prep time: 10 minutes | Cook time: 2 hours minutes | Serves 4

Indulge in the delightful flavors of coconut and cherry with our Fast Coconut and Cherry Tea Loaf. This recipe offers a quick and easy way to create a moist and flavorful loaf that will impress your taste buds. With just 10 minutes of preparation time and 2 hours of cooking, you'll have a delicious treat ready to be enjoyed.

To begin, gather your ingredients, including starter (fed, unfed, or discarded), coconut milk, white spelt flour (plain or all-purpose flour), glacé (candied) cherries, dried cranberries, shredded coconut, runny honey, a large egg, baking soda, and baking powder. In a medium-sized mixing bowl, combine all the ingredients and mix them thoroughly until a lumpy, thick batter forms, ensuring there are no dry flour pockets remaining.

Spoon the batter into a prepared loaf pan, and then it's time to decide whether you prefer to bake in a preheated oven or from a cold start. If preheating, set your oven to 350°F (180°C) for convection or 400°F (200°C) for conventional. Bake the loaf uncovered for 50 to 60 minutes if using a preheated oven or set a timer for 60 minutes if using a cold start. Insert a metal skewer or thin knife into the center of the loaf to check for doneness; it should come out clean.

During the baking process, keep an eye on the loaf's browning. If the top starts to brown too quickly, cover the pan with another pan upside down or with a piece of foil. Once baked, remove the loaf from the oven and the pan, taking off the parchment paper or liner. Allow the loaf to cool on a wire rack before serving, savoring the aroma of coconut and cherries.

The Fast Coconut and Cherry Tea Loaf is perfect for a cozy afternoon tea or as a delightful dessert. Its moist texture and fruity flavors make it a crowd-pleasing treat for any occasion. Enjoy it freshly baked, or store it in an airtight container for later indulgence. With its simplicity and deliciousness, this tea loaf recipe is sure to become a staple in your baking repertoire.

- 100 g (½ cup) starter (fed, unfed or discarded)
- 400 g (1¾ cups) coconut milk
- 400 g (2½ cups) white spelt flour, plain or all-purpose flour
- 200 g (1¼ cups) glacé (candied) cherries
- 100 g (¾ cup) dried cranberries
- 50 g (½ cup) shredded coconut
- 30 g (⅛ cup) runny honey
- 1 large egg
- 7 g (1 tsp) baking soda
- 4 g (½ tsp) baking powder

1. In a medium-sized mixing bowl, combine all the ingredients. Mix them well to form a lumpy, thick batter, ensuring no dry flour is left. It will fill the bowl.
2. Spoon the mixture into your prepared loaf pan.
3. When you are ready to bake, decide whether you would like to bake in a preheated oven or from a cold start. If preheating, set the oven to 350°F (180°C) for convection or 400°F (200°C) for conventional.

1. If you preheated the oven, bake the loaf uncovered for 50 to 60 minutes, or until a metal skewer or thin knife inserted into the center comes out clean. If you are using a cold start, place the uncovered pan of dough in the oven, set the temperature as above and set a timer for 60 minutes. Bake it for the allotted time, or until a metal skewer or thin knife inserted into the center comes out clean.
2. If the top of the loaf starts to overly brown, cover the pan with another pan upside down over the top, or with a piece of foil.
3. Remove the pan from the oven and the loaf from the pan, removing the parchment paper or liner and placing it uncovered on a rack. Allow it to cool before serving.

Chapter 8
Pan Loaves

Sandwich Bread

Prep time: 20 minutes | Cooking time: 50 minutes | Serves 1

Welcome to the world of artisanal baking! Sourdough bread, with its distinct tangy flavor and rustic charm, has captivated the taste buds of bread enthusiasts for centuries. This recipe offers you a delightful opportunity to embark on a journey of creating your very own sourdough masterpiece. Whether you're an experienced baker or just starting your bread-making adventure, this recipe will guide you through the process with precision and care.

Sourdough bread is a perfect choice for those seeking a wholesome and hearty loaf. The fermentation process, fueled by natural wild yeast present in the sourdough starter, not only imparts a unique flavor but also enhances the bread's digestibility and nutritional value. It requires patience and attention to detail, but the reward is well worth the effort.

In terms of pairing suggestions, sourdough bread harmonizes beautifully with a wide array of toppings and spreads. From classic combinations like avocado and poached eggs to more adventurous pairings like smoked salmon and cream cheese, this versatile bread is a canvas for culinary exploration. Its robust crust and chewy interior make it an ideal base for sandwiches, toasts, or simply enjoyed on its own.

During the production process, it's crucial to handle the sourdough starter with care, as it serves as the heart and soul of the bread. Maintaining the right balance of hydration, temperature, and feeding intervals will contribute to a successful fermentation. Additionally, proper kneading and shaping techniques will help achieve an open crumb structure and an appealing artisanal appearance.

So, let's roll up our sleeves, gather our ingredients, and embark on this sourdough adventure together. Get ready to experience the satisfaction of creating your very own delicious and nourishing sourdough bread. Let's dive in!

- 1 1/3 cups scalded milk
- 2 tablespoons unsalted butter
- 2 tablespoons honey
- 2 teaspoons salt
- 4 1/4 cups all-purpose or bread flour
- 3/4 cup sourdough starter
- 1 tablespoon milk

1. Scald the milk by warming it to 180°F in a microwave or on the stove. Because of evaporation, you may want to start with 330 grams of milk.
2. Add the butter, honey, and salt to the hot milk to dissolve them, then chill the mixture in the refrigerator down to about 90°F. This should take about 15 minutes.
3. Combine the flour, sourdough starter, and milk mixture in a medium bowl and mix thoroughly. Transfer the dough to a floured countertop and knead it by hand for 2 to 3 minutes.
4. Cover the dough and let it bulk ferment for 6 to 12 hours at room temperature, or until it has just about doubled in size.
5. Flour your countertop, scrape the dough out onto it, and shape the dough into a tube.
6. While the dough rests on its seam, lightly oil your loaf pan, then place the dough in the pan, seam-side down.
7. Cover and proof the dough for 2 to 4 hours. You can also retard the dough in the refrigerator overnight or longer. The dough is ready to bake when it has doubled in size or its highest part crests over the lip of a 9-by-5-by-2¾-inch loaf pan.
8. Place one of your oven racks in the second-from-the-bottom position. Preheat your oven to 350°F for about 15 minutes.
9. Brush the milk on the top of the loaf and put the pan in the oven.
10. Bake for 45 to 50 minutes, or until the interior of the loaf is over 190°F.
11. When the bread has finished baking, immediately remove it from the pan. Cool it on a rack on its side to discourage settling of the crumb for at least 1 hour before slicing.
12. Once completely cooled, store the bread in a plastic bag or beeswax wrap to keep it soft.

Sourdough Naan

Prep time: 4 hours 30 minutes | Cook time: 4 hours 38 minutes | Makes 8 pieces

Indulge in the irresistible flavors of Sourdough Naan, a delightful twist on the traditional Indian flatbread. This recipe invites you to explore the realm of sourdough baking while savoring the pillowy texture and aromatic essence of freshly made naan. Whether you're a seasoned sourdough enthusiast or new to the world of fermentation, this recipe promises a satisfying culinary adventure.

Crafting the perfect Sourdough Naan requires careful attention to detail, starting with activating the sourdough starter. By combining the starter with lukewarm water and flour, you awaken the wild yeast and set the foundation for a flavorful dough. Allow this mixture to rest and develop its character for 6 to 12 hours before moving on to the next step.

Once the starter is activated, it's time to prepare the bread dough. The combination of whole-wheat flour, all-purpose flour, baking powder, and a touch of fine sea salt creates a balanced and textured base for your naan. Mixing the active starter with warm milk, Greek yogurt, and melted butter infuses the dough with moisture and richness. Kneading the dough until it becomes supple and elastic is key to achieving the perfect consistency.

After a four-hour rise, divide the dough into individual portions and let them rest. Preheat your griddle or cast iron skillet to the optimal temperature and roll each dough ball into thin, round pieces. The magic happens as you cook the naan, brushing them with melted butter for a luscious golden finish. The naan should bubble and develop a slight char, resulting in a soft interior and a slightly crisp exterior.

The versatility of Sourdough Naan knows no bounds. Pair it with your favorite curries, dips, or use it as a base for creative wraps and sandwiches. These delectable breads can also be frozen, ensuring you always have a batch ready to enjoy whenever the craving strikes.

As you embark on this sourdough naan journey, remember to savor each step and revel in the process of creating something truly special. From activating the starter to rolling out the dough and witnessing the transformation on the cooking surface, you'll experience the joy of homemade naan like never before. So gather your ingredients, ignite your passion for baking, and let's dive into the world of Sourdough Naan together.

TOOLS NEEDED:

- stand mixer, flattop griddle or cast iron skillet, pastry brush
- For Activating The Starter:
- 4¾ ounces (½ cup) sourdough starter
- 4 ounces (½ cup) lukewarm (90°f to 100°f) pure filtered or bottled water
- 4 ounces (1 cup) whole-wheat flour or (scant 1 cup) unbleached all-purpose flour
- For The Bread Dough:
- 4 ounces (1 cup) whole-wheat flour
- 4¼ ounces (1 cup) unbleached all-purpose flour
- 1 teaspoon baking powder
- ½ teaspoon fine sea salt
- 9½ ounces (1 cup) active sourdough starter
- 4 ounces (½ cup) warm (100°f to 125°f) milk
- 4⅓ ounces (¼ cup) nonfat greek yogurt
- 2 ounces (½ stick) butter, melted and cooled, divided
- olive oil, for coating the dough

TO ACTIVATE THE STARTER:

1. At least 6 to 12 hours before making the dough, in a medium bowl, combine the starter, lukewarm water, and flour, completely incorporating the ingredients into the starter. Loosely cover and let sit on the counter until ready to use.

TO MAKE THE BREAD DOUGH:

2. In the bowl of a stand mixer fitted with a dough hook, or a large bowl, stir together the whole-wheat flour, all-purpose flour, baking powder, and salt.
3. In a small bowl, whisk the active starter, milk, yogurt, and 1 tablespoon of melted butter. Add the wet ingredients to the dry ingredients and mix on low speed, or stir by hand, to combine. The mixture will be stiff. Knead the dough on low speed for at least 5 minutes, or 10 minutes by hand. Lightly coat the outside of the entire dough ball with a bit of olive oil. Cover the bowl with a clean damp kitchen towel and let rise for 4 hours.
4. Lightly flour a breadboard or clean work surface and turn the dough out on to it. Divide the dough into 8 pieces. Cover the dough with a clean kitchen towel and let rest for 30 minutes.
5. Preheat your griddle or cast iron skillet over medium-high heat.
6. Using a floured rolling pin, roll each dough ball into a thin, round piece, about ¼ inch thick.
7. Sprinkle a couple drops of water onto the cooking surface. When the water sizzles, it's time to cook the naan. Using a pastry brush, brush one side of the dough pieces with some of the remaining 3 tablespoons of melted butter and place 2 pieces at a time, buttered-side down, into the skillet. As soon as the edges bubble, about 1 minute, brush the top of the naan with melted butter. Turn to cook on the other side. The naan should be done in about 2 minutes. Repeat to cook all the naan.
8. Naan freezes beautifully. Place it in an airtight resealable freezer bag for freezing, where it will keep for up to three months.

Whole Wheat Pan Loaf

Prep time: 20 minutes | Cooking time: 50 minutes | Serves 1

Welcome to the world of wholesome and nourishing bread with our Whole Wheat Pan Loaf recipe. This delightful loaf is a celebration of whole grain goodness, combining the rich flavors of whole wheat flour and the tangy notes of sourdough. As a professional chef, I'm excited to guide you through this recipe, offering helpful tips and insights to ensure your baking success. This Whole Wheat Pan Loaf is perfect for those who appreciate the hearty flavors and health benefits of whole grains. It's an ideal choice for everyday enjoyment, whether you're looking to elevate your morning toast, create wholesome sandwiches, or simply savor a slice on its own.

To create this delicious loaf, we start by building a whole grain sourdough starter, which adds depth and complexity to the bread's flavor profile. The scalded milk, honey, and butter mixture lend a touch of sweetness and moisture to the dough, creating a tender crumb. With careful attention to the dough's fermentation and proofing stages, we ensure optimal rise and texture.

As you embark on this baking adventure, remember to handle the dough with care, providing ample time for fermentation and proofing. The loaf develops a beautiful golden crust and a soft interior, making each bite a delight for your senses. Once cooled, store the bread properly to maintain its freshness and enjoy it over the following days.

Get ready to experience the satisfaction of creating a wholesome, homemade loaf that will fill your kitchen with the comforting aroma of freshly baked bread. Let's dive into the process and create a Whole Wheat Pan Loaf that will nourish both body and soul.

- 1 2/3 cups scalded milk
- 2 tablespoons unsalted butter
- 2 tablespoons honey
- 2 teaspoons salt
- 4 cups whole grain flour
- 3/4 cup sourdough starter
- 1 tablespoon milk

1. Approximately 4 to 8 hours before you want to start mixing your dough, build a whole grain sourdough starter by taking ½ teaspoon of your existing starter and mixing it with 35 grams of whole grain flour and 35 grams of water. (After the starter's expansion has peaked, feed it again if you need more starter or want the starter to have even less of the original all-purpose flour.) Note that the starter will ferment a little faster than refined flour starter, and it'll have fewer surface bubbles due to a weaker gluten network.
2. Scald the milk by warming it to 180°F in the microwave or on the stove. Because of evaporation, you may want to start with 400 grams of milk.
3. Add the butter, honey, and salt to the hot milk to dissolve them, then chill the mixture in the refrigerator down to about 90°F. This should take about 15 minutes.
4. Combine the flour, starter, and milk mixture in a medium bowl and mix thoroughly. If you find this dough too wet to knead by hand, let it rest for 15 to 30 minutes and give it a round of stretching and folding (see step 2 in the Cinnamon Raisin Light Wheat Pan Bread recipe).
5. Cover the dough and let it bulk ferment for 6 to 12 hours at room temperature, or until it has just about doubled in size.
6. Flour your countertop, scrape the dough out onto it, and shape the dough into a tube.
7. While the dough rests on its seam, lightly oil your loaf pan, then place the dough in the pan seam-side down.
8. Cover and proof the dough for 2 to 4 hours. The dough is ready to bake when it has doubled in size or its highest part crests over the lip of a 9-by-5-by-2¾-inch loaf pan.
9. Place one of your oven racks in the second-from-the-bottom position. Preheat your oven to 350°F for about 15 minutes.
10. Brush the milk on the top of the loaf and put the pan in the oven.
11. Bake for 45 to 50 minutes, or until the interior of the loaf is over 190°F.
12. When the bread has finished baking, immediately remove it from the pan. Cool it on a rack on its side for at least an hour before slicing.
13. Once completely cooled, store the bread in a plastic bag or beeswax wrap to keep it soft.

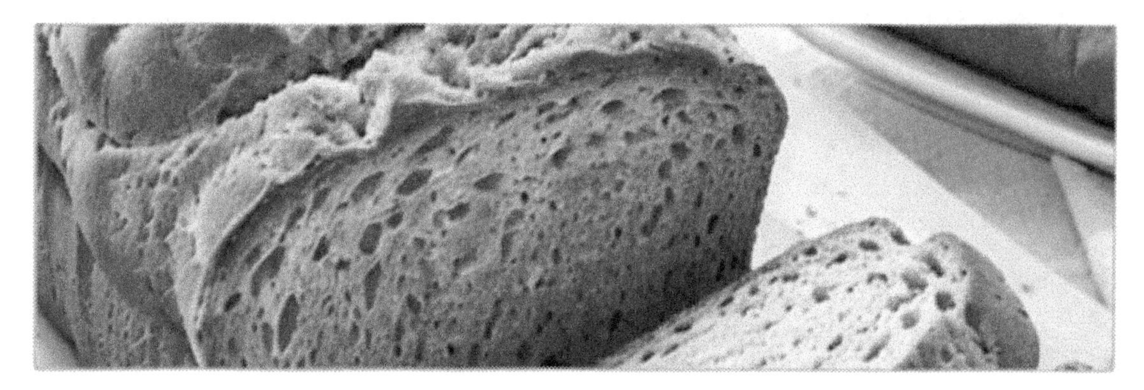

Cinnamon Raisin Light Wheat Pan Bread

Prep time: 20 minutes | Cooking time: 50 minutes | Serves 1

Indulge your senses with the warm and comforting aroma of freshly baked Cinnamon Raisin Light Wheat Pan Bread. As a professional chef, I'm delighted to guide you through the creation of this delightful bread, which combines the wholesome goodness of whole grain and the sweet allure of cinnamon and raisins.

This recipe is perfect for those seeking a bread with a touch of sweetness and a hint of spice. The combination of all-purpose or bread flour and whole grain flour creates a light and tender crumb, while the sourdough starter adds depth and complexity to the flavor profile. The addition of cinnamon and plump raisins takes this bread to the next level, providing bursts of sweetness and texture in every bite.

To begin, we'll thoroughly mix the flours, water, sourdough starter, honey, salt, and cinnamon, ensuring that the raisins are evenly distributed throughout the dough. This step prevents the dried fruit from clumping together or leaving dry pockets in the bread. We'll then let the dough rest briefly before giving it a gentle round of stretching and folding to enhance its structure.

During the bulk fermentation stage, the dough will rise and develop its distinct flavor and texture. Once doubled in size, we'll shape the dough into a loaf and let it proof until it reaches its desired size. You have the option to proof the dough at room temperature or refrigerate it overnight for a more developed flavor.

As the bread bakes to a beautiful golden brown, your kitchen will be filled with the irresistible aroma of cinnamon and raisins. The finished loaf should be cooled on its side to maintain its structure and moisture, allowing the flavors to settle.

This Cinnamon Raisin Light Wheat Pan Bread is perfect for breakfast or as a tasty snack throughout the day. Savor it on its own, lightly toasted with a smear of butter, or transform it into delectable French toast. Store the bread properly to ensure its freshness and enjoy it for several days.

Let's embark on this baking journey together, creating a loaf of Cinnamon Raisin Light Wheat Pan Bread that will bring joy to your table and delight your loved ones.

- 2 3/4 cups all-purpose or bread flour
- 1 1/3 cups whole grain flour
- 1 1/2 cups water
- 3/4 cup sourdough starter
- 2 tablespoons honey
- 2 teaspoons salt
- 2 teaspoons cinnamon
- 1 cup raisins

1. Thoroughly mix the flours, water, starter, honey, salt, and cinnamon in a medium bowl. Add the raisins and continue mixing until they're evenly distributed. (Separating the mixing into two steps prevents dry flour from getting trapped in the crevices of the dried fruit.)
2. Cover and let the dough rest for 15 minutes, then give it a round of stretching and folding: With damp fingertips, stretch and fold the dough, lifting the edge of one side of the dough and folding it over to the other side. Go around the bowl two or three times, stretching and folding each side, and stop when the dough feels tighter.
3. Let the dough bulk ferment for 6 to 10 hours at room temperature, or until it has just about doubled in size.
4. Flour your countertop, scrape the dough out onto it, and shape the dough into a tube.
5. Cover and proof the dough for 2 to 4 hours. You can also retard the dough in the refrigerator overnight or longer. The dough is ready to bake when it has doubled in size or its highest part crests over the lip of a 9-by-5-by-2¾-inch loaf pan.
6. Place one of your oven racks in the second-from-the-bottom position. Preheat your oven to 350°F for about 15 minutes.
7. If the top of your dough isn't damp already, brush or spray water on it. You may want to score this dough to control the oven spring.
8. Bake for 50 minutes, or until the interior of the loaf is over 190°F.
9. When the bread has finished baking, immediately remove it from the pan. Cool it on a rack on its side (to discourage settling of the crumb) for at least 1 hour before slicing.
10. Once completely cooled, store the bread in a plastic bag or beeswax wrap to keep it soft.

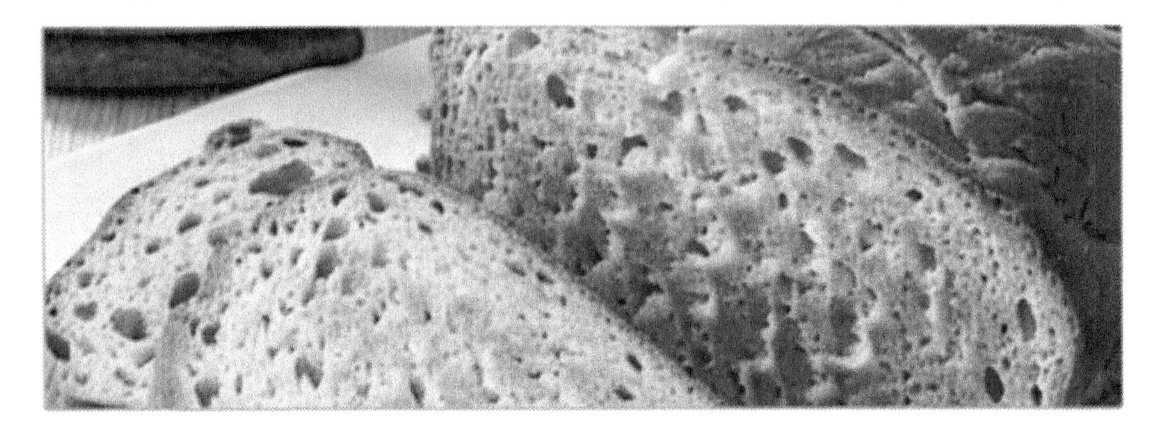

Buckwheat Pan Bread

Prep time: 20 minutes | Cooking time: 50 minutes | Serves 1

Buckwheat Pan Bread - a delightful and wholesome recipe that combines the unique nuttiness of buckwheat flour with the tangy flavors of sourdough. This recipe is perfect for those seeking a hearty and nutritious bread option. With its rustic texture and rich flavors, this Buckwheat Pan Bread is an excellent choice for various occasions.

Buckwheat flour adds a distinct earthy taste and enhances the nutritional profile of the bread. It is gluten-free and packed with fiber, protein, and essential minerals. The combination of all-purpose or bread flour and buckwheat flour provides a balanced texture and depth of flavor.

The Buckwheat Pan Bread pairs wonderfully with both sweet and savory accompaniments. Enjoy it toasted with a dollop of honey or spread it with your favorite nut butter for a delightful breakfast. For a savory twist, use it to create delicious sandwiches or serve alongside hearty soups and stews.

When working with the dough, note that the buckwheat flour may result in a slightly wetter consistency. If needed, allow the dough to rest and perform a round of stretching and folding to improve its structure. This step ensures a well-developed and cohesive dough.

This recipe is perfect for those who appreciate the unique flavors and health benefits of buckwheat. It caters to individuals seeking a gluten-free or fiber-rich bread option. Whether you're looking for a nutritious homemade bread for everyday enjoyment or a special occasion, the Buckwheat Pan Bread will satisfy your cravings.

Prepare to indulge in the warm and comforting aroma of freshly baked bread as you follow these simple steps. The end result is a beautifully golden loaf with a crisp crust and a soft, moist crumb. Enjoy the Buckwheat Pan Bread at any time of the day, knowing that you've created a wholesome and flavorsome bread from scratch.

- 3 1/3 cups all-purpose or bread flour
- 3/4 cup buckwheat flour
- 1 1/4 cups water
- 3/4 cup sourdough starter
- 1/4 cup plus 1 tablespoon plain yogurt
- 2 teaspoons salt

1. Combine the flours, water, sourdough starter, yogurt, and salt in a medium bowl and mix thoroughly. If you find this dough too wet to knead by hand, let it rest for 15 to 30 minutes and then give it a round of stretching and folding: With damp fingertips, lift the edge of one side of the dough and fold it over to the other side. Go around the bowl two or three times, stretching and folding each side, and stop when the dough feels tighter.
2. Cover the dough and let it bulk ferment for 6 to 10 hours at room temperature, or until it has just about doubled in size.
3. Flour your countertop, scrape the dough out onto it, and then shape the dough into a tube. This dough is on the west side, so you may need to roll the dough a second time.
4. While the dough rests on its seam, lightly oil your loaf pan, then place the dough in the pan seam-side down.
5. Cover and proof the dough for 2 to 4 hours. You can also retard the dough in the refrigerator overnight or longer. The dough is ready to bake when it has doubled in size or its highest part crests over the lip of a 9-by-5-by-2¾-inch loaf pan.
6. Place one of your oven racks in the second-from-the-bottom position. Preheat your oven to 350°F for about 15 minutes.
7. Dust the top of the dough with flour and score down the center. This dough tends to expand during baking, and a score will prevent a rupture on the side of the loaf.
8. Bake for 50 minutes, or until the interior of the loaf is over 190°F.
9. When the bread has finished baking, immediately remove it from the pan. Cool it on a rack on its side (to discourage settling of the crumb) for at least 1 hour before slicing.
10. Once completely cooled, store the bread in a plastic bag or beeswax wrap to keep it soft.

New York Deli Rye Pan Bread

Prep time: 20 minutes | Cooking time: 50 minutes | Serves 1

New York Deli Rye Pan Bread – a classic and flavorful bread that pays homage to the iconic delis of New York City. This recipe combines the rich flavors of whole grain rye flour, the tanginess of sourdough, and the aromatic touch of caraway seeds. With its hearty texture and distinctive taste, this New York Deli Rye Pan Bread is perfect for recreating the authentic deli experience in your own kitchen.

The combination of all-purpose or bread flour and whole grain rye flour creates a well-balanced dough with a robust flavor profile. The addition of caraway seeds adds a delightful aroma and complements the rye perfectly. The sourdough starter provides a tangy undertone and enhances the bread's texture.

The New York Deli Rye Pan Bread is a versatile option that pairs exceptionally well with a variety of deli-inspired fillings. Create delicious sandwiches with pastrami, corned beef, or smoked salmon. Alternatively, serve thick slices alongside pickles, sauerkraut, and mustard for a classic deli platter. The robust flavors of this bread make it an ideal choice for hearty and satisfying meals.

Due to the sticky and wet nature of the dough, it is recommended to let it rest and perform a round of stretching and folding to improve its structure. This step ensures a well-developed and cohesive dough, even though it may be challenging to knead by hand.

This recipe is perfect for those seeking to recreate the authentic flavors of a New York deli at home. The New York Deli Rye Pan Bread is a must-have for sandwich enthusiasts, rye bread lovers, or anyone looking to add a touch of nostalgia to their meals. Whether you're planning a casual lunch, a picnic, or a family gathering, this bread will elevate your culinary experience.

Prepare to be transported to the bustling streets of New York City as you savor the aroma and taste of freshly baked New York Deli Rye Pan Bread. With its distinct flavors and chewy texture, this bread will undoubtedly become a favorite among your friends and family. Enjoy the pride and satisfaction of serving a homemade bread that captures the essence of a true deli classic.

- 2 3/4 cups all-purpose or bread flour
- 1 1/4 cups whole grain rye flour
- 1 1/3 cups water
- 3/4 cup sourdough starter
- 2 tablespoons honey
- 2 tablespoons olive oil
- 1 1/2 tablespoons caraway seeds
- 2 teaspoons salt

1. Combine the flours, water, starter, honey, oil, caraway seeds, and salt in a medium bowl and mix thoroughly. This dough is too sticky and wet to knead by hand, but you can let it rest for 15 to 30 minutes and then give it a round of stretching and folding: With damp fingertips, lift the edge of one side of the dough and fold it over to the other side. Go around the bowl two or three times, stretching and folding each side, and stop when the dough feels tighter.
2. Cover the dough and let it bulk ferment for 6 to 10 hours at room temperature, or until it has just about doubled in size.
3. Flour your countertop, scrape the dough out onto it, and shape the dough into a tube.
4. While the dough rests on its seam, lightly oil your loaf pan, then place the dough in the pan seam-side down.
5. Cover and proof the dough for 2 to 4 hours. You can also retard the dough in the refrigerator overnight or longer. The dough is ready to bake when it has doubled in size or its highest part crests over the lip of a 9-by-5-by-2¾-inch loaf pan.
6. Place one of your oven racks in the second-from-the-bottom position. Preheat your oven to 350°F for about 15 minutes.
7. Brush or spray water on the top of the dough if it isn't damp already.
8. If you haven't let your dough expand as much as recommended in step 5, then score it to control the oven spring.
9. Bake for 50 minutes, or until the interior of the loaf is over 190°F.
10. When the bread has finished baking, immediately remove it from the pan. Cool it on a rack on its side to discourage settling of the crumb. Give this loaf at least 2 hours to cool before slicing because rye bread needs more time to set, or solidify.
11. Once completely cooled, store the bread in a plastic bag or beeswax wrap to keep it soft.

Chapter 9
Biscuits, Bagels, Buns, Rolls, and More

Bacon and Cheese Biscuits

Prep time: 10 minutes | Cook time: 20 minutes | Makes 10 to 12 biscuits

Experience the irresistible combination of smoky bacon, savory cheese, and flaky biscuits with our Bacon and Cheese Biscuits recipe. These homemade delights are quick to prepare and deliver a comforting indulgence that will leave your taste buds craving more. Perfect for breakfast, brunch, or as a delightful addition to any meal, these biscuits are sure to become a family favorite.

Bacon and Cheese Biscuits are an ideal choice for various scenarios. Whether you're hosting a weekend brunch, preparing a delicious grab-and-go breakfast, or simply craving a warm and savory treat, these biscuits will elevate any occasion. The savory combination of bacon and cheese creates a delightful balance of flavors, making them a great accompaniment to soups, stews, or even enjoyed on their own as a snack.

These biscuits are the perfect blend of savory ingredients. The addition of crispy bacon and tangy cheddar cheese adds a burst of flavor to every bite. Serve them alongside scrambled eggs and fresh fruit for a satisfying breakfast. For a brunch gathering, pair them with a creamy mushroom or spinach quiche. Enjoy them warm with a dollop of honey or your favorite jam for a delightful sweet and savory combination.

To achieve tender and flaky biscuits, it's important to keep the butter cold while mixing it into the dry ingredients. Working quickly with a pastry cutter or fork will help maintain the desired texture. Gently kneading the dough a few times ensures proper incorporation of the ingredients without overworking the dough, resulting in tender biscuits.

When shaping the dough, remember to flatten it to about 1 inch thick for a proper rise during baking. Using a floured biscuit cutter or sharp knife, cut the dough into individual biscuits. Placing the biscuits on a lined baking sheet ensures even baking and easy cleanup.

During baking, keep a close eye on the biscuits to achieve a puffed and golden appearance. Adjust the baking time as needed based on your oven's temperature. The aroma of these biscuits will fill your kitchen, indicating they're ready to be enjoyed.

With our Bacon and Cheese Biscuits recipe, you can savor the warm and comforting flavors of bacon and cheese in every bite. These biscuits are a delightful addition to any meal or occasion. So, gather your ingredients, preheat the oven, and get ready to enjoy the deliciousness that awaits.

- 1 cup unbleached all-purpose flour
- 2 tsp. baking powder
- ½ tsp. baking soda
- ¼ tsp. salt
- ⅓ cup very cold butter, cubed
- ¾ cup shredded cheddar cheese
- 8 slices bacon, cooked, cooled, and crumbled
- 1 cup active starter

1. Preheat the oven to 425°. Line a baking sheet with a silicone baking mat or parchment paper; set aside for now.
2. In a medium mixing bowl, whisk together the flour, baking powder, baking soda, and salt. Using a pastry cutter or fork, mix in the butter until mixture has coarse crumbles, working quickly so the butter doesn't get too warm. Mix in the cheese and bacon. Next, add ¾ cup of the starter and mix until a soft dough forms, adding the remaining starter if needed.
3. Turn out the dough onto a floured work surface and gently knead a few times. Using your hands or a rolling pin, flatten the dough to about 1 inch thick. Using a floured biscuit cutter or a sharp knife, cut it into 10 to 12 biscuits. Place the biscuits on the prepared baking sheet and bake for 12 to 15 minutes or until puffed and golden.

Soft Share and Tear Rolls

Prep time: 5 minutes | Cook time: 15 minutes | Makes 12 soft rolls

Indulge in the warm and comforting goodness of our Soft Share and Tear Rolls. These delightful rolls are incredibly soft, making them perfect for sharing and tearing apart with loved ones. With a simple and quick preparation process, these rolls will be ready to grace your table in no time. Whether enjoyed as a side dish, used for sandwiches, or simply savored on their own, these soft rolls are sure to please.

Soft Share and Tear Rolls are a versatile addition to various scenarios and special occasions. Whether you're hosting a casual family gathering, planning a picnic, or preparing a delicious sandwich platter for a party, these rolls will impress your guests with their tender texture and delightful taste. Their shareable nature fosters a sense of togetherness, making them a perfect choice for cozy family meals or communal dining.

To ensure the desired softness and fluffiness, it's important to handle the dough with care. When mixing the dough in a stand mixer, gradually add the warm milk mixture to achieve the right consistency. The dough will be wet and sticky, resembling cake batter. Resting the dough allows it to develop flavor and structure.

During the second rise, ensure the rolls are placed in a well-coated baking pan to prevent sticking. The dough should be lightly floured to facilitate shaping into a rectangle and then cut into 12 equal pieces. Gently roll each piece into a ball and arrange them in the pan. The rolls should be given adequate time to rise, resulting in a puffy appearance.

Before baking, brush the rolls with an egg wash for a shiny and golden finish. Adjust the baking time based on your oven, aiming for fully risen and rich golden brown rolls.

Once baked, these Soft Share and Tear Rolls are best enjoyed warm or at room temperature. They can be stored in a plastic bag at room temperature for up to 2 to 3 days, ensuring they stay fresh and delicious.

With our Soft Share and Tear Rolls recipe, you can create a batch of delectable rolls that are perfect for sharing and tearing apart. Gather your ingredients, follow the simple steps, and get ready to savor the irresistible softness of these delightful rolls.

DOUGH:

240 g (1 cup) milk, whole or 2%
60 g (¼ cup) water
28 g (2 tbsp) unsalted butter, cubed, plus more for coating
1 large egg
200 g (1 cup) bubbly, active starter
24 g (2 tbsp) sugar
450 g (3¾ cups) bread flour
5 g (1 tsp) fine sea salt
Egg Wash:
1 large egg
splash of water

MAKE THE DOUGH:

1. In a small saucepan, warm the milk, water, and butter over low heat or in the microwave. Cool slightly before adding to the dough.
2. Meanwhile, add 1 egg, starter, and sugar to the bowl of a stand mixer fitted with the paddle attachment. Mix on low speed to combine. Gradually add the warm milk mixture, followed by the flour and salt. Continue to mix until a wet and sticky dough forms, about 1 to 2 minutes. The texture will look very similar to cake batter. When finished, scrape down the sides of the bowl. Cover and let rest for 30 minutes. Replenish your starter with fresh flour and water, and store according to preference.
3. After the dough has rested, switch to the dough hook and knead on medium-low speed, about 6 to 8 minutes. The dough will not come together in a ball but will look shiny and smooth when ready. Scrape down the sides of the bowl once more.

BULK RISE:

1. Transfer the dough to a new bowl lightly coated in butter. Cover the dough and find a warm spot for it to rise. This could be near a heater, on top of the fridge, or even in a cabinet. Let it rest until double in size, about 6 to 8 hours, depending on temperature.

SHAPE:

1. Lightly coat a 9 × 13-inch (23 × 33-cm) baking pan with butter.
2. Remove the dough onto a lightly floured surface. With floured fingertips, gently flatten into a rectangle. Cut the dough into 12 pieces, about 85 grams (3 oz) each, with a floured knife or bench scraper. Gather the ends, flip the dough over, and roll each piece into a ball. Place into your pan, 3 pieces across and 4 down.

SECOND RISE:

1. Cover the pan with a damp towel and let rest for 1 hour or more, depending on temperature. The dough should look puffy, but not fully risen, when ready. Alternatively, cover the dough with lightly oiled plastic wrap and chill overnight, up to 8 hours. Return to room temperature before baking, about 1 hour.
2. Preheat your oven to 400°F (200°C). Combine the remaining egg with a splash of water. Brush the tops of the dough for a shiny finish.

BAKE:

1. Bake the rolls on the center rack for about 35 to 40 minutes. The rolls will be fully risen and rich golden brown when finished. Serve warm or at room temperature, family-style, to share and tear.
2. Soft rolls will last up to 2 to 3 days. Store in a plastic bag at room temperature to maximize freshness.

Quick Biscuits

Prep time: 10 minutes | Cook time: 20 minutes | Makes about 8 biscuits

When you're craving warm and flaky biscuits in a hurry, our Quick Biscuits recipe comes to the rescue. These delightful biscuits require minimal prep time and are made with simple pantry ingredients. With their buttery goodness and tender texture, these biscuits are sure to become a family favorite. Whether served as a side dish, enjoyed with a dollop of butter and jam, or used as a base for breakfast sandwiches, these quick biscuits will satisfy your cravings in no time.

Quick Biscuits are a versatile addition to various scenarios and special occasions. Whether you're hosting a weekend brunch, preparing a quick breakfast on a busy morning, or craving a comforting accompaniment to your favorite soups and stews, these biscuits fit the bill. Their simplicity and deliciousness make them suitable for casual gatherings, family meals, or even picnics.

The Quick Biscuits recipe yields biscuits with a golden exterior and a tender, flaky interior. Serve them warm alongside your favorite breakfast items such as eggs, bacon, or sausage for a satisfying morning meal. They also pair well with soups, stews, and chili, providing a comforting and flavorful addition to your lunch or dinner. For a sweet treat, top these biscuits with whipped cream and fresh berries or drizzle them with honey or maple syrup.

To achieve the best results with your Quick Biscuits, it's important to handle the dough properly. Cut the butter into small cubes and keep it very cold to create those coveted flaky layers. Use a fork or pastry cutter to incorporate the butter into the flour mixture until it resembles coarse crumbs. This step ensures the butter is evenly distributed, resulting in a tender texture.

When adding the starter to the flour mixture, mix it with a spoon until the flour is mostly combined. Then, knead the dough in the bowl with your hands until it comes together. Avoid overmixing, as this can lead to tough biscuits.

When rolling out the dough, aim for a thickness of ¾ inch. Use a floured biscuit cutter or a sharp knife to cut the biscuits. Gather any scraps and reroll them to make the most out of the dough.

Depending on your preference, you can arrange the biscuits on the baking sheet with the sides touching for softer biscuits or spread them out for crisper sides. Adjust the baking time accordingly, aiming for a golden brown color and a fully baked interior.

Once baked, these Quick Biscuits are best enjoyed fresh out of the oven or within a few hours. Serve them warm for the ultimate flakiness and flavor.

With our Quick Biscuits recipe, you can whip up a batch of delectable biscuits in no time. Their simplicity and versatility make them a go-to option for various occasions. Prepare a tray of these quick biscuits and delight in the warm, flaky goodness that will surely please everyone at the table.

- 1 cup unbleached all-purpose flour or bread flour
- 2 tsp. baking powder
- ½ tsp. salt
- ½ tsp. baking soda
- 6 t. very cold butter, cut into small cubes
- 1 cup starter (discard is fine)

1. Preheat the oven to 425°.
2. In a medium mixing bowl, whisk together the flour, baking powder, salt, and baking soda. Cut the butter into the flour mixture using a fork or pastry cutter until the mixture looks like coarse crumbs. Add the starter and mix with a spoon until the flour is mostly combined. Knead the dough in the bowl with your hands for a minute or so until the dough comes together.
3. Turn out the dough onto a floured work surface and then roll or pat it to ¾ inch thick. Cut the biscuits with a floured biscuit cutter or sharp knife. Gather the scraps together, roll them out again, and cut more biscuits to get as many as possible. (I usually end up with a smaller, misshapen biscuit at the end, but it tastes just as good as the pretty ones!)
4. Place the biscuits on an ungreased baking sheet, either spread out for crisper sides or with the sides touching for softer biscuits.
5. Bake for 12 to 15 minutes or until done. (If the biscuits are touching, it may take a few more minutes for them to fully bake.)

Easy Pita Pockets

Prep time: 5 minutes | Cook time: 15 minutes | Makes 8 pitas

Welcome to the delightful world of Easy Pita Pockets! This recipe is designed for those seeking a convenient and satisfying meal option that combines the goodness of sourdough with the versatility of pita bread. Whether you're a busy professional looking for a quick lunch or a home cook seeking a wholesome and homemade alternative to store-bought pitas, this recipe is sure to please.

The beauty of these Easy Pita Pockets lies in their simplicity. With just a handful of ingredients and straightforward steps, you'll be rewarded with soft, fluffy, and flavorful pitas that can be filled with your choice of ingredients. Let's dive into the details.

Before we begin, make sure you have an active and bubbly sourdough starter, as it plays a crucial role in creating that delightful tangy flavor. The dough itself comes together effortlessly, with a combination of all-purpose and whole wheat flours, warm water, a touch of honey for subtle sweetness, and a drizzle of olive oil for a hint of richness.

Once the dough is prepared, it undergoes a gentle rest to develop its structure and flavor. During this time, you can replenish your starter, ensuring its vitality for future baking endeavors. After the rest, it's time for the dough to rise, doubling in size to achieve that sought-after lightness.

Shaping the pita pockets is an enjoyable process that involves dividing the dough into individual portions and rolling them into neat balls. This is followed by a brief second rise, where the dough relaxes and becomes puffy, ready for the next step.

Now, it's time to roll out the dough into thin circles. A dusting of flour ensures a smooth rolling experience, and with each circle, you'll witness the pitas come to life, transforming from simple dough rounds to airy pockets ready to be baked.

Speaking of baking, a hot cast iron skillet or pizza stone provides the perfect surface for achieving those characteristic pita bubbles. The baking process is quick, requiring only a few minutes per pita. Keep a watchful eye to prevent overcooking, as the pitas puff up rapidly and develop a desirable golden color.

Once baked, transfer the pitas to a wire rack to cool slightly. While they may deflate a bit, their delightful texture remains intact. These sourdough pitas can be stored in a plastic bag for several days, allowing you to enjoy them at your convenience.

Whether you choose to fill these Easy Pita Pockets with fresh veggies, hummus, or your favorite protein, they serve as a versatile canvas for creating a variety of delectable meals. From quick and wholesome lunches to satisfying dinner options, these pitas will surely become a staple in your culinary repertoire.

So, roll up your sleeves and embark on a delightful journey of baking Easy Pita Pockets. With their homemade charm and irresistible flavor, these pitas are bound to bring joy to your table and satisfy your cravings with each delicious bite.

- ½ cup bubbly, active starter
- ¾ cup warm water
- 1 teaspoon honey
- 1 tablespoon olive oil
- 1 ¼ cups all-purpose flour
- 1 cup whole wheat flour
- ½ teaspoon fine sea salt

MAKE THE DOUGH:

1. In a medium bowl, whisk the starter, water, honey, and olive oil together with a fork. Add the flours and salt. Mix to combine, then finish by hand until a rough dough forms. Cover with a damp towel and let rest for 30 to 45 minutes. Replenish your starter with fresh flour and water, and store according to preference.
2. After the dough has rested, work the mass into a semi-smooth ball, about 20 seconds.

BULK RISE:

1. Cover the dough and let rise at room temperature, 70°F (21°C), until double in size, about 6 to 8 hours.

SHAPE:

1. Line a sheet pan with parchment paper and set aside. Remove the dough onto a lightly floured work surface. Divide into 8 pieces, about 65 grams (2¼ oz) each. Pinch the ends, flip the dough over, and roll each piece into a ball. Place onto your sheet pan, seam side down.

SECOND RISE:

1. Cover the dough with a damp towel and let rest until puffy, about 30 minutes to 1 hour. Meanwhile, preheat your oven to 450°F (230°C). Place a cast iron skillet or pizza stone on the bottom rack to heat up.

ROLL THE DOUGH:

1. Generously dust your work surface with flour, then dust the tops of the dough. Working with one ball of dough at a time, roll into a thin circle about ¼ inch (6.3 mm) thick (see tip below). If using a pizza stone, roll out a second ball of dough to bake 2 rounds at a time.

BAKE:

1. Place the dough into your hot skillet and bake for about 3 to 4 minutes. Pitas puff up quickly and cook fast, so keep your eye on them. When finished, transfer to a wire rack; they will deflate slightly as they cool. Finish rolling and baking the rest of the pitas.
2. These sourdough pitas will stay fresh in a plastic bag for up to 3 to 4 days at room temperature.

Appendix 3 Index

N

O

P

R

S

T

U

V

W

Y

Z

PATRICIA C. MEADORS

9 781805 381679

Printed by BoD™in Norderstedt, Germany